For the year 2017, Plant Construction Company LP has, along with Heyday, participated in producing *Lost Worlds of the San Francisco Bay Area,* written by Sylvia Linsteadt. This is the twenty-eighth successive annual book that we have distributed as a gift to our friends and customers. *Lost Worlds* features Bay Area places, people, and activities that most readers, even those who have lived here all of their lives, will know little or nothing about. History books often tell us about well-remembered events, such as the Earthquake and Fire of 1906 or World Wars I and II, as well as extraordinary people and their achievements. This book shifts our attention to some of the forgotten people of the past and how they worked, played, and attempted to recover their health during some of these same time periods. It tells of everyday hardships and everyday abundance off the main road, and it testifies to the impermanence of seemingly permanent places that came and went in their time.

We hope you will enjoy this look at the past and feel inspired to compare the photographs and descriptions of the lost worlds herein with what exists at those same locations today.

We wish you a healthy, happy, and prosperous New Year.

David Plant
January 2017

Lost Worlds of the San Francisco Bay Area

Sylvia Linsteadt
Foreword by Gary Kamiya

Heyday. Berkeley. California

Library of Congress Cataloging-in-Publication Data

Names: Linsteadt, Sylvia, author.
Title: Lost worlds of the San Francisco Bay Area / Sylvia Linsteadt ;
    foreword by Gary Kamiya.
Description: Berkeley, California : Heyday, [2017]
Identifiers: LCCN 2016031666 | ISBN 9781597143912 (hardcover : alk. paper)
Subjects: LCSH: San Francisco Bay Area--Description and travel. |
    Industries--California--San Francisco--History. | San Francisco Bay Area
    (Calif.)--History.
Classification: LCC F869.S3 L25 2017 | DDC 979.4/6--dc23
LC record available at https://lccn.loc.gov/2016031666

Cover photo courtesy of the Mill Valley Public Library History Room
Back cover photo courtesy of the Getty's Open Content Program
Book Design: Ashley Ingram
Map: David Deis
Map font from the Fell Types, digitally reproduced by Igino Marini, www.iginomarini.com
Victorian ornaments designed by Tommy Firmansyah

Orders, inquiries, and correspondence should be addressed to:
        Heyday
        P.O. Box 9145, Berkeley, CA 94709
        (510) 549-3564, Fax (510) 549-1889
        www.heydaybooks.com

Printed in China by Regent Publishing Services, Hong Kong

10 9 8 7 6 5 4 3 2 1

To the many peoples of the Bay Area, past, present, and future.
May we remember to steward the lands we live on with pride and love.

CONTENTS

FOREWORD

Gary Kamiya

The Bay Area is one of the most extraordinary places on earth. It features one of the greatest harbors on the planet, the largest inland delta, and one of the world's most beloved cities. It's the global center of technological innovation. And its Mediterranean climate, ideal latitude, and vast network of green spaces and parks allow it to sustain an astonishing cornucopia of animal and vegetable life.

These things are obvious. But some of the Bay Area's most remarkable treasures are hidden from view. They are the once-vibrant places that now exist only in memory—lost worlds obscured by the passage of time, like overgrown ruins. Yet it only takes a little historical excavating, plus the rarer gift of imagination, and these places appear again, as vivid and irreducible as they once were, unexpected gifts from the past. Sylvia Linsteadt's book brings eighteen of those lost worlds to life.

And what strange and wonderful worlds they are! After years of exploring the obscure byways of San Francisco and Bay Area history, I'm a fairly hard person to surprise. But no less than three of the chapters in this book are about places I had never heard of—the Arequipa Sanitorium in Fairfax, where working-class female tuberculosis patients made pottery in the early twentieth century as a therapeutic intervention; the Belgum Sanitarium on Wildcat Canyon Road, where wealthy patients suffering from "nervous disorders" (or drug addiction) were stashed away in the bucolic East Bay hills; and the whaling station at Point Molate in Richmond, which amazingly did not close until 1971. After reading this book, my mental map of the area will never be the same.

But Linsteadt does more than unearth obscure facts. Her greatest achievement is to make the past breathe—to evoke the atmosphere of a bygone time. Take the opening of her chapter on the side-wheel steamers that ran between San Francisco and Sacramento starting during the gold rush. It's no great achievement to look up those steamers and describe what kind of crafts they were, how many passengers they carried, when they stopped running, and so on. But capturing what it felt like to be the riverboat pilot on one of those steamers on a late summer night, with the moon illuminating the tule reeds, navigating by dim landmarks such as a distinctive cottonwood tree or an old adobe, while the engine throbs and a few insomniacs wander the decks, that is something else altogether—something closer to what San Francisco's most illustrious hack, who chose the name Mark Twain in homage to his beloved profession of riverboat pilot, did in *Life on the Mississippi*.

Such epiphanic descriptions pop up throughout this book, and every time they do, they blaze a trail that cuts through the dark forest of the past, each one illuminating its subject like a bonfire in a clearing. From the magical never-never land of Alameda's Neptune Beach, which in Linsteadt's effervescent telling seems even more wondrous than San Francisco's more famous Playland at the Beach, to the majestic stands of old-growth redwoods that once existed in one small area of the Oakland hills before they were cut down in an orgy of greed that Linsteadt aptly compares to the gold rush itself, to the inconceivably rich—and toxic—New Almaden quicksilver mine near San Jose, where the Cornish inhabitants of "Englishtown" adorned a coast oak with initialed boxes into which their cuts of meat were delivered by the meat wagon, this book is a rich and varied remembrance of things past.

And yet to remember is not always to celebrate. Some of the things that Linsteadt writes about here were wonderful, such as the overflowing treasure trove that was the old Emporium department store or the apricot trees that once perfumed the Santa Clara Valley, but others were deplorable, like the destruction of some of the planet's greatest trees or the whaling trade that almost drove the magnificent mammals to extinction. But all of these lost worlds, both good and bad, once existed, and what gives this book its electric charge is that they existed right next to us. They deserve to be remembered, for they are part of our common heritage. They helped make our area, our world, and our selves what we are.

But we don't need moral or pedagogical reasons to immerse ourselves in these worlds. Knowing about them simply makes our lives richer, deeper, and stranger. By pulling these long-forgotten objects out of the attic trunks where they were buried, dusting them off, and displaying them with such care that they shine again, Sylvia Linsteadt has broadened our present by opening it to a dimension filled with inconceivable treasures: the past.

Gary Kamiya is the author of the best-selling book *Cool Gray City of Love: 49 Views of San Francisco* and he writes a history column for the *San Francisco Chronicle* titled "Portals of the Past."

Introduction

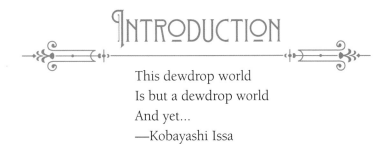

> This dewdrop world
> Is but a dewdrop world
> And yet...
> —Kobayashi Issa

With these words, and a list of about twenty-five initial subjects, Heyday's founder Malcolm Margolin pulled the inspiration for *Lost Worlds of the San Francisco Bay Area* out of thin air— as he is wont to do—and laid it lovingly in my care. I have long been a lover and a student of history, and of the forgotten stories of the Bay Area where I was born and raised. But the opportunity to write this book took me down new pathways. Or perhaps, better put, along forgotten old roads—up Mount Tamalpais in a steam train; among the apricot blossoms in the valley where Google now flourishes; into the hills above Fairfax to a sanatorium where pottery was made by tubercular women; up the Sacramento River in a paddlewheel boat, watching a sky of unfathomable stars; into the clanging metal shipyards of Sausalito during World War II; along the oxcart-rutted roads of the Mexican ranchero days.

The result is a book of brief but luminous meditations on eighteen "lost worlds" throughout the Bay Area, selected for the cadence of the material, and the potential therein for story, for poetry, for imagination. I should be clear here that though these chapters are heavily researched and therefore accurate in all of their particulars, they are also acts of historical imagination. I am a novelist as much as I am a historian and naturalist, and so I tried to put myself in the shoes of the people who inhabited these various times and places with as much sensitivity and immediacy as I could, while still remaining faithful to historicity and fact.

These "dewdrop worlds" roughly span the geography of the Bay Area, from its outer northern edge at Fort Ross—which, though technically beyond the boundaries of what we now consider the Bay, was connected enough via trade to San Francisco that it warranted inclusion—extending all the way south to the New Almaden quicksilver mine, east as far as Mount Diablo's Black Diamond mine, and west to the Farallon Islands.

What you will not find here are "lost worlds" that predate the arrival of the Spanish in the 1770s. Grouping, say, the precontact myth-telling traditions of the Huchuin Ohlone, or the millennia-old dance ceremonies of the Coast Miwok, with twentieth-century whaling at Point Molate felt wrong. More than wrong, it felt downright offensive, and misguided too. A culture irrevocably altered by conquest, conversion, exploitation, and racism is not what we mean by a "lost world" in this book. The rich, astoundingly beautiful, and long-sustained indigenous cultures of the Bay Area are not dewdrops. They are taproots. They are whole root systems and geologies and ecosystems, and, perhaps most importantly, they are also *not* lost, because Coast Miwok and Ohlone and Pomo people are still here, doing the difficult but beautiful and life-affirming work of reclaiming language, dance, basketry, and story.

But dozens of other, smaller human worlds have come and gone in the Bay Area since Europeans arrived, and all in the blink of an eye. Coal mining, a railroad up Mount Tamalpais, a sanatorium for tubercular girls, San Francisco's own bohemia—all dewdrops that we have mostly forgotten, that have been swept up in the great tide of change that defines what it means to be human in this world despite all of our attempts to preserve, amend, protect, defend, or downright *stop* the currents of time and transformation that are as inevitable, in the end, as plate tectonics. When change stops, the world stops. Or, as Rainer Maria Rilke writes in one of his *Sonnets to Orpheus,* "What tightens into survival is already inert." In this book, I have tried to celebrate what is ephemeral, to remind us of the many gleaming moments of beauty and human dignity threaded through the past. To tell some of their stories. Doing so makes my understanding of this present ephemeral moment—writing from a sunny morning window in Oakland—that much more rooted, oriented in a web of other dewdrops.

In these chapters I have tried to keep things away from simple dichotomies between good and bad; I've tried to bring to life the humanity of the Bay Area's many complicated histories. To help us imagine what it might have been like to go down into the Mount Diablo coal mines daily because it was the only work available to you; to invoke the smells and sights of forgotten apricot orchards in summer, or a lighthouse among Pacific storms and the screaming of murres. To help reorient and remind us that there are stories everywhere underfoot. That the block you live on didn't always look like that—in fact, it's probably only very recently looked like that. While I may have my personal opinions about mercury mines or whaling stations, the purpose of this book is not to beat you over the head with those opinions, but to step out of the way in order to show you glimpses of other realities that once existed right here.

While it is true that the world changes and we can do nothing to stop it, we *can* have a hand in shaping that change toward good. It has been said many times that the better we understand the past, the better we can understand the present, and the more likely we are to avoid repeating our mistakes. The better we understand the stories and the worldviews and the materials that created the built environments and cultural mindsets in which we dwell, the more capable we are of moving into an ecologically threatened future with a sense of depth, a sense of place, a sense of story and possibility, and perhaps above all a sense of hope in the potential of the human spirit to create beauty, not destruction. May we all seek to approach the world thus—as a place of overwhelming wonder and also inevitable transformation, where there are always new dewdrops to discover, clinging at dawn to every leaf.

A whaling scene. From *The Marine Mammals of the Northwestern Coast of North America*, by Charles Melville Scammon, 1874

Point Molate Whaling Station

They left the docks at Richmond's Point Molate before dawn with harpoon guns loaded, heading west for the Farallones or south to the waters off Monterey. Everyone's livelihood depended on the aim of the gunner, as the whole crew was paid per foot of whale. Harpoon guns carried a charge that exploded inside the whale's body, after which the carcass was inflated for buoyancy like a terrible silver balloon and strapped to the side of the boat. Some days might yield four whales; others might be entirely lost to a wild chase across open water. Freshly caught meat had to be hightailed back to the whaling station at Point Molate to prevent the bodies from rotting, and the journey sometimes took ten hours, boats strapped with whales like haunting buoys.

Even though he had a knack for it and made a comfortable living too, ex–harpoon gunner Pratt Peterson told KQED during an interview that he never felt completely at ease with the killing of whales because he felt too much in awe of them—how wise their old and wrinkled eyes, how, dragged up out of the sea, they were beings of impossible majesty. And yet for him and hundreds of other men at Point Molate, work was work, and so you put the smell, and the twist of doubt, somewhere below your heart, out of mind.

The whaling station at Point Molate, perched at the far western edge of Richmond, was the last of its kind in the United States and operated from 1956 to 1971 by the Del Monte and Golden Gate fishing companies. Sperm, humpback, fin, and sei whales hunted in the open ocean were processed here into dog and cat food, poultry feed, and spermaceti, an oil highly prized in the weapons industry as a lubricant for missile guiding systems.

In the early days, tens of thousands of whales migrated off the coast of San Francisco twice each year—up to forty thousand per season, according to the observations of nineteenth-century whaler and mariner Charles Melville Scammon. From the mid- to late-1800s, the San Francisco Bay was the largest whaling port on the West Coast, and the main refinery, Arctic Oil Works, flourished on Illinois Street between Sixteenth and Seventeenth Streets in San Francisco.

An illustration of the Arctic Oil Works headquarters in San Francisco, where whales were processed for oil and baleen throughout the 1800s and into the early 1900s. Courtesy of The Bancroft Library

There, the oil of whales as well as seals and sea lions was processed. Whale oil was used not only to lubricate various forms of machinery, from train pistons to factory cogs; it was also an important and cheap source of light. The oil lit the streets and homes of old San Francisco, giving off a not entirely pleasant scent in the process. Humpback whales were particularly prized by California whalers because of the amount of oil in their blubber. In an era just before electricity, whale oil was used as the main lubricant in all industrial operations. It lit the headlamps of the miners in the Black Diamond mines. It was used in soap and candle making.

Top left: A hunter at the whaling gun on an Oakland trawler in 1927. Courtesy of the San Francisco History Center, San Francisco Public Library

Top right: Whales were spotted from the crow's nest, and the catch always depended on how good the lookout was. Photograph taken 1927. Courtesy of the San Francisco History Center, San Francisco Public Library

Bottom right: A whale laid out along a gangway. Courtesy of the New Bedford Whaling Museum

Whalebone baleen was processed into commercial goods such as corsets and umbrellas in the Pacific Steam Whaling Company yard. Photograph circa 1890. Courtesy of the New Bedford Whaling Museum

Inset: A bloated whale being hoisted up a slipway collapsed from overuse at Point Molate. Photograph by John Caito Sr.

The rare ambergris found only in the intestines of the less common sperm whales (produced, it is thought, to help ease the digestion of sharp or rough meals such as the beaks of giant squid) was as prized as pearls for its fixative properties in the perfume industry. The boning in corsets and skirt hoops was made from baleen.

It is extraordinary, and devastating, to imagine cityscapes lit by the bodies of the great wise whales of the ocean depths, to imagine women in their corsets breathing shallow against the pressure of baleen.

Gray and humpback whales in the Pacific Ocean were hunted to the brink of extinction to fuel the cities up and down the edge of the continent during the whaling heyday of the late nineteenth and early twentieth centuries.

Point Molate was the last of this lineage, though the era of oil lamps and corsets was long gone. Back at the docks, a crew of forty men boasted that they could reduce a humpback whale—somewhere around fifty feet in length and weighing forty tons—to oil, pet food,

The last fin whale to enter the tryworks at Point Molate's whaling station in 1968.
Courtesy of the San Francisco Maritime National Historical Park

Above: Moby Dick brand whale meat sold for general consumption.

Right: Moby Dick brand whale meat pet food.

Both images courtesy of John Caito Sr.

and poultry meal, in under an hour and a half. This was not an easy or a safe undertaking. The amount of blood and oil produced when cutting out the blubber was of such a volume that the processing area would become slick with it. If more than one whale had been brought in during the day's hunt, they were processed one by one, the others left in the shallows to keep fresh. The whalers used grappling hooks to drag the giant carcasses up the gangplank from the shallows by their tails, and employed blades as big as floor sweepers (according to one bystander) to carve off the skin and fat. The blubber was pulled free with more hooks and lowered into giant cookers, where it was rendered into oil. Meat and bones were ground up and sent off to big pet and poultry feed companies, such as Moby Dick Pet Food, which advertised its product as "lean red meat high in protein." And so an entire whale was transformed into tins of mass-produced meat, meal and oil, and the humpbacks and finbacks, sperms and seis killed year by year teetered closer to extinction.

Meanwhile, under the ocean's skin, the old songs that humpbacks had sung to each other for millennia were finally being heard by the likes of Western

Men with giant slabs of baleen standing outside the counting rooms of William Lewis & Sons in San Francisco circa 1905.
Courtesy of the New Bedford Whaling Museum

scientists, particularly two environmentalists and oceanographers, Robert Payne and Scott McVay, who in the late sixties made the first recordings of what they argued could only be whale *song* (as opposed to simple noise)—elaborate vocalizations that lasted twenty minutes to an hour, full of repeating notes and refrains, and different from season to season, community to community. The whale became a mascot for the early environmental movement—a symbol of the effects of the rampant destructions of the twentieth century, and a reminder of the mysteries yet to be discovered in this great and vast world. In 1972, Congress passed the Marine Mammal Protection Act, and Point Molate's whaling station was abandoned, just a set of dock

The true cost of whaling, shown in piles of bones in Monterey circa 1896. Courtesy of the New Bedford Whaling Museum

Opposite page: Humpback whales leaping and breaching. From *The Marine Mammals of the Northwestern Coast of North America,* by Charles Melville Scammon, 1874

pilings and the memory of blubber and bones, haunted, perhaps, by old and sorrowing songs.

Close to extinction by the seventies, humpbacks and grays have rebounded so well since whaling was banned in this country that they are no longer considered threatened. Every year they undertake enormous migrations—from the Gulf of Alaska to Baja California, crossing three thousand miles of ocean each way in the process. The wet, dark back of a humpback rising through the waves in wintertime is a flash of something primordial. Perhaps it is the great size of the gray and humpback whales that pass our shores every year that catches at our hearts, that inspires people to gather in droves on January afternoons out at Point Reyes Lighthouse, shivering while holding up a pair of binoculars and gasping, at last, at the sight of a glinting back, a spout of water, a slapping tail, or perhaps the gift of a whole breach. Or perhaps it's the knowledge that these barnacle-encrusted giants are also milk-making, warm-blooded mammals like ourselves, yet they swim and sleep and eat in the ocean, a realm forever mysterious and marvelous to us.

But they still don't travel as close to shore as they once did, due to the trauma of the whaling years. It's as if an old warning about harpoons and travel routes is still being passed on from mother to child, perhaps in song, just in case.

A Marinship tanker being towed to an outfitting dock by a little "yard tug." Courtesy of the Sausalito Historical Society

MARINSHIP

For three years, warships were born along the Sausalito waterfront like so many colossal beasts. And, befitting such behemoths, their births required hundreds of midwives: men and women who crawled and climbed, soldered and nailed, painted and tiled, all over their enormous bodies. They took great pride in a job well done as their beasts sailed from the Marinship harbor in Sausalito and out through the Golden Gate, freshly painted and bedecked with crisply waving flags. Otis R. Williams, a painter, told an oral-history film crew that he always brought his wife and daughters down to the waterfront to see the ship he'd just finished, each brushstroke of paint a source of satisfaction. "Well, I had something to do with the finishing of that ship," he'd always say—as one of his daughters told the film crew for *Marinship Memories* more than half a century later—proud to know each curve and join, inside and out, from kitchen to captain's bridge to engine room to stern. He put a bit of himself into each paint job, knowing it was the ship's final skin, knowing it would weather unfathomable waves and storms, and possibly enemy fire too.

Each time a ship was finished, and all the steel ties binding it to the yard were cut loose, thousands of people rushed to the waterfront to watch it being christened. Most of the spectators, dressed in their best hats and shoes, cheering and waving the steel beasts off on their journeys, were the families of the hundreds of workers who had made the ship. The wife of a Marinship executive broke a bottle of champagne (wound tight with red, white, and blue ribbons) on the hull in a rush as the ship pulled away. A long latticework of shadows from the enormous scaffolding towers rippled along its fresh gray sides in the late afternoon light as it pushed out into open water, using a deep channel dredged to accommodate the hulls of tankers. A test voyage around the bay, and all the way out past the rugged and desolate Farallon Islands, was run by the men and women who had built the ship. Upon return, a notch was made in a broom and the broom was hoisted all the way up the rigging—for the first successful journey, and many more to come.

Above: "Bow art" on a Marinship tanker, painted on each ship at its launch celebration.

Left: The wives of Marinship executives breaking bottles of champagne to christen the hull of SS *Whittier Hills*.

Opposite page: SS *Mission San Francisco* was the ninety-third and last ship launched from Marinship's docks. The ceremony was held September 18, 1945.

All photographs courtesy of the Sausalito Historical Society

Six tankers on the shipways, all under construction at once. Courtesy of the Sausalito Historical Society

When people think of the wartime shipbuilding industry in the Bay Area, their thoughts usually go to the Kaiser Shipyards in Richmond, where as many as three ships were built each day. A total of 747 ships were built in Richmond by the end of World War II, more than at any shipyard anywhere in the world. The Rosie the Riveter Memorial lives today in one of its historic yards. The story of Marinship, and the community that it birthed, is less known.

At Marinship, as many as six ships might be under construction at once, lined up inside their pillars of scaffolding along the bay's edge. Giant yellow cranes were at the ready to lift and lower enormous pieces of steel, like a 115-ton engine room foundation, or a 17-ton propeller, in one go. Here, men and women in blue and white work clothes swarmed the hulls and sterns, the engines, cabins, and decks, like bees. The place ran with all the efficiency of a hive, the ships extensions of the people who, in a flurry of focused and skilled labor, welded them together, from the laying of the hull to the last piece of furniture affixed to the captain's cabin.

The creation of Marinship itself was an enormous undertaking. After the attack on Pearl Harbor, the Bechtel Corporation funded and, with astonishing rapidity, built a shipyard right on the rich marsh edge of Sausalito. It was a good launching place out to the Golden Gate and onward to the theaters of war, and it was one of the last undeveloped stretches of bay edge big enough to accommodate a shipyard. A neighborhood was bulldozed, marshlands were flattened and filled, native burial sites and the quiet homes of ducks were torn up by the mouths of giant bulldozers. Just a few months after Pearl Harbor, workers were building warships at Marinship. It made for a very stark contrast: the martial hulls of Liberty ships and oil tankers shadowed by a forest of scaffolding above, and behind them, the silhouette of Mount Tamalpais, wooded and serene. Between them, the mile-long rows of warehouses housed a veritable library of every shape and size and cut of steel imaginable and little buses and vans ferried pieces of metal around the thoroughfares. In the bay beyond—iridescent at sunrise, stalked by white egrets—every so often a harbor seal might pop up to peer at the giant ships with dark and curious eyes.

A very early glimpse of the Marinship yard, with only Liberty ships at the outfitting dock. Courtesy of the Sausalito Historical Society

People flocked to the shipyard, drawn by good wages. The promise of $1.30 an hour, a weekly wage elsewhere, was a strong incentive. Men often struck out first to test the waters, and a great flood of African American men came by train from Louisiana and Alabama—sometimes sitting out the whole crowded ride in an aisle on their suitcases. They called for their families to join them if the going was good, and wives and children rushed to follow, women taking jobs alongside their husbands. Male labor was scarce during World War II, and women made up 25 percent of the Marinship workforce, many of them seeking work as single women independent of husband and family. Here, Rosie the Riveter was born, among the strong women doing work that had been previously restricted to men.

Top: A line of people waiting to apply for jobs at Marinship, which attracted workers from many different backgrounds and walks of life.

Bottom: Women worked alongside men at Marinship, and were proud of their jobs. Here, Mamie Ray Thompson, Ethel Davidson, Ann Hudson, and Mabel Hilbert pause their welding to pose for a photo. Both photographs courtesy of the Sausalito Historical Society

Marin City was planned in three days and built in several weeks by the US government to house workers and their families. By the end of 1943, it was the largest town in Marin County. Courtesy of the Sausalito Historical Society

Some seventy-five thousand people worked for Marinship by 1945, so many that a whole town was built to house them—Marin City. Homes were arranged like the warehouses in the shipyard, box-shaped and neatly lined up in identical rows. But it was a good life, and longtime residents remembered it fondly. Shifts ran around the clock, so there were always workers com-

ing and going along the mile stretch to the shipyard. In *Marinship Memories*, former workers reminisced that nobody locked their house, and neighbors knew one another's schedules and looked out for each other. If one woman's laundry was out on the line and it started to rain while she was at work, a neighbor took it down and brought it inside for her. The milkman left his delivery just inside. Everyone had the shipyard in common, and conversation ran long into the night, or the lunch hour, about which ship you were working on, how far along it was, the budding romance between this pipe cutter and that flanger, the band that played at lunchtime last week, whether or not the foreman was drunk on the job last Tuesday morning.

But the work wasn't without its dangers. Even though Marinship boasted the best safety record in the country, and had a well-equipped hospital on site, building tankers was risky work, especially at the feverish pace demanded by the war. Scaffolds broke and people fell

Above: The hull of a Liberty ship surrounded by elaborate scaffolding.

Left: A cover cartoon for *The Marin-er* magazine poking fun at the obvious dangers of working in a shipyard.

Both images courtesy of the Sausalito Historical Society

to their deaths. Men climbed up hooks on the cranes to help attach them, often without any safety nets or ropes. A falling wrench, a loose piece of steel plummeting from great heights could be deadly. Ship painters hung from ropes over the bay to coat the exterior

Women workers at Marinship hoist the Tanker Champs flag with pride after beating all other US shipyards in the production of tankers in March 1944. Courtesy of the San Francisco History Center, San Francisco Public Library

Inset: On the top level of the mold loft and yard office was a giant open space for laying out plywood templates, which were later used to mark steel sheets for ship parts. Courtesy of the Sausalito Historical Society

and sometimes suffered an accidental dunk in the cold water. Sometimes, people came to work drunk. The injured and dead alike were carried out on stretchers, and Annie Small told oral historians how her mother-in-law always got a peek at the hands of the mortally wounded, to make sure it wasn't someone she loved.

It was serious work, work that took a confidence and precision of body and mind. Rodessa Battle, a friend of Annie Small, was told upon arrival: "You gotta go up this ladder if you want to work on this ship." Well, she went up that ladder, and as she says, "I've been goin' up there ever since." If you had a fear of heights, you were put to different work—welding, for example, or

painting, pipe cutting or flanging. Women wearing eye shields and work pants welded steel alongside men, and got so good at it that Small claimed she could "do it in her sleep." It was easy to get flying bits of steel lodged in your eyes if you weren't careful and severe burns on your arms. But for those used to making mere pennies an hour, it was worth the trouble and the danger. Besides which, it was satisfying to watch raw materials take form under your hands, from the giant copper pipes twice as tall and wide as men to the insulation and electrical wiring carefully lining every cabin. It was exhilarating to use hands and mind to turn so much metal into massive, sleek ships made in

Tankers lined up along the Marinship harbor, as seen from the bay. Courtesy of the Sausalito Historical Society

Three Marinship workers: Martha Gaskins, a skilled burner; Gentry Moore, a chipper; and Rudolph Sims, a shipfitter journeyman who worked on the skids. Courtesy of the Sausalito Historical Society

the name of God and country. This was an era of optimism, of binary thinking—good and evil, peace and war—and to build a ship that would carry the oil to refuel Allied powers abroad made people proud; it gave meaning to their days that many never forgot.

Around the Bay Area, especially in Richmond at the Kaiser Shipyards, African American communities grew and thrived, and solidarity ran high. But the shipyards were not without racial tension, and Marinship was no exception. White employees were quick to exclude black colleagues from trade organizations such as the local Boilermakers union. Workers fought back and, with the *James v. Marinship* Supreme Court case in 1944, won African Americans equal opportunity to join unions, and therefore access to equal pay.

At the end of the war, the shipyard vanished as quickly as it was created, and with it went tens of thousands of jobs. But Marin City remained, as did the vibrant community of men and women who had the memories of warships in the muscles of their arms. Now, only a few elderly women remain who remember the shipyard days firsthand, women who could still cut pipes in their sleep. To them, Marinship was a time of purpose and of peace, when neighbors looked out for each other, when young men worked together, and did not live in poverty or fear. "I just wish for everybody to get along again," says Rodessa Battle, "but I don't think I'm going to see that, not in my lifetime."

Looking east from the changing rooms across the giant pool before the expansion of Neptune Beach onto bay fill in the mid 1920s. Courtesy of Chuck Millar

Neptune Beach

Neptune Beach was open only a short time, a brief interlude of impossible fullness and ostentation between the two world wars. It was a dream that flourished and then vanished just as fast as a lucky spin on the wheel of fortune. You entered through lit archways, past a ten-story, octagonal-roofed tower that loomed like some Moorish dream. One silver dime got you a whole day of glorious fun. Beyond the gates sprawled the Street of Damascus, the main promenade where a labyrinth of concession booths boasted all the prizes you could dream of, and many you could not: teapots, sugar bowls, Kewpie dolls, clocks inside toy ships, goldfish, and canaries guaranteed to sing. At one stand, a man held a fistful of strings in his hand. Each string was attached to a prize hanging from the ceiling. You gave the fellow a coin and pulled one of the strings, hoping to win the best prize of the lot, the embroidered satin Chinese jacket that caught the light so beautifully just above you. But that string was tucked deep inside the man's palm, while all the others dangled within your reach. You might tug the whole handful and never win that tantalizing jacket.

It was a magnificently sprawling complex of diversions and attractions. There were the two giant, bay-fed pools: one saltwater, one fresh; the Whoopee roller coaster snaked in wild loops along the edge of Alameda, carrying its riders through the sky and giving them stark, crystalline views of San Francisco; the countless concession stands with their prizes (mostly) rigged to remain just out of reach, like that gleaming jacket; the high-diving competitions and baseball games and wrestling matches; the tiny trained monkeys that raced cars around a miniature speedway, looking preposterously human and wild at once. And that was only the beginning.

Neptune Beach grew out of a decades-long tradition of city folk seeking sunshine along Alameda's coastline. Since the 1870s the area had been a beach resort destination for city- and fog-weary souls from San Francisco, and those fleeing the heat further inland. It was easy to reach from the city via a ferry and the Southern Pacific Transportation Company train, known as the red train, which together amounted to a forty-minute journey. Several smaller bathhouses had flourished more modestly along the bayfront pre-Neptune, such as Terrace Baths and Garden Baths, which were frequented by famous literary visitors as Jack London and Robert Louis Stevenson.

But when the Strehlow family bought the eighty-seven acres of beach property at Alameda's West End in 1917, they combined the ethos of the older beachside bathing resorts—made for relaxation and rejuvenation—with a penchant for the whimsy, carnivalesque play, and dazzling engineering feats of a newer American tradition: the amusement park. Robert Strehlow was a senior partner at Strehlow, Freese & Peterson, the premier amusement park contractor in the United States, responsible for numerous world's fairs, including the Pan-American Exposition in 1901 and the Alaska-Yukon-Pacific Exposition in 1907. Strehlow had been responsible too for the construction of many of the pavilions at the Panama-Pacific International Exposition in 1915, which briefly turned San Francisco's Marina district into a "Jewel City," a distillation of the art, celebrity, and natural wonders of the whole world. Both the spirit and the look of Neptune were born in the wake of the exposition's enchantment.

Above: The famous Moorish tower at the entrance to Neptune Beach.

Left: A crowd inside the front entrance to the park during the grand opening of the Neptune Palace Theater.

Opposite page: The eponymous Neptune on an iconic postcard. The image was used on the park's early stationery.

All images courtesy of Chuck Millar

A crowd of beachgoers in fine dress. Courtesy of Chuck Millar

As its name suggests, Neptune Beach was a world apart, and woven through every inch of the place was a thread of the gaudy divinity of a lost—or perhaps never quite achieved—age; to call it either a beach resort or an amusement park hardly does the place justice. It was both, and more. From 1917 until 1939, all manner of entertainments flourished in this sprawling playground, many of them created from pieces left over when the fantastically elaborate Panama-Pacific International Exposition was taken down. The most notable was a German carousel hand carved by Gustav Dentzel—complete with mythical hippocampi (creatures part horse, part dolphin) that pulled the sea-god Neptune's chariot, not to mention ostriches, giraffes, deer, roosters, tigers and more—and bought by Neptune for $35,000. The Scenic Railway roller coaster and the shooting gallery were also dismantled and barged across the bay to grace Neptune's grounds.

Above: An early beach scene before the park was extended into the bay.

Right: Neptune Beach tickets. All images courtesy of Chuck Millar

Billed as the "Coney Island of the West," Neptune Beach drew a crowd of twenty thousand through its gates on opening day, a crowd the gleaming new park was well equipped to handle. There were dressing rooms to accommodate eight thousand bathers, a pavilion large enough to hold fifteen thousand, and two enormous swimming pools (one 300 feet long, the other a whopping 575), not to mention the fine, sandy beach along the bay, and the dizzying maze of

entertainment venues. It's hard to imagine how it all fit, with the crowds of revelers strung throughout like thousands of merry lights. Perhaps the whole place shifted and spun around its visitors like some funhouse of strange and magnifying mirrors—here, a horse-racing arena, there, a ballroom-dance competition stage; here a wrestling ring, there a restaurant with food from all over the world; here a masquerade ball, there a small village of concession stands where you might, after emptying your pockets of change, win a prize or two.

There was plenty of room to picnic—and picnicking was a very popular thing to do on that fine, sandy beach—and vendors abounded in every direction, hawking hot dogs and popcorn, chocolates, cotton candy, ice cream, and Epsicles (the prototype of the popsicle, named for its supposed inventor, a young man named Frank Epperson who created the treat on a very cold San Francisco night). Strehlow was always dreaming up new entertainments and commissioning new rides to keep his visitors satisfied. In 1925, the *Alameda Times-Star* featured an article about the Swan Flier, a new ride handmade in Berlin. Beautiful wooden swans lifted their riders into the air and swung about, dipping and wheeling, their hinged wings flapping as if in flight.

While it was, in the end, all fun and games, some of the games were more serious than others—professional baseball was hosted in an eight-thousand-seat stadium, and champion swimmers competed and set records, among them Duke Kahanamoku and Helen Crlenkovich. On the beach, more playful, but no less competitive, games ensued, such as greased pole

Top: A little boy climbing a pole greased for contests, with the dining hall and dance pavilion in the background, circa 1923.

Bottom: Highwire bicycling over the pool, a daredevil promotion to get people to visit the park.

Both photographs courtesy of Chuck Millar

Top: Swimmers diving into the pool.

Bottom left: Women in bathing attire outside the showers, with the dining hall in the background and the pool to the right.

Bottom right: The exterior of the Safety Racer ride, photographed from Central Avenue. This L. A. Thompson ride was purchased from the Panama-Pacific International Exposition and brought to Alameda by barge.

All photographs courtesy of Chuck Millar

A panorama of Neptune Beach after the expansion of the 1920s, with the second, larger pool and picnic area to the right and the vacation cottages in the background. Courtesy of Chuck Millar

climbing and canoe tilting, where men and women tried to capsize one another's boats with their oars. Beauty contests were held down by the water and featured demure ladies in striped bathing costumes holding elegant parasols—at least, according to some photographs. According to one advertisement, however, the competitions weren't always so demure: "Dainty dolls in the latest creations. It only took three stitches to make some of their bathing suits and if the wearer sneezes—zowie—good night."

When it began to fall apart, it fell apart fast. Three stitches loose and it was gone—zowie! During the twenties, Strehlow had expanded Neptune Beach elaborately, creating a separate area called Kiddieland, which was like Neptune in miniature, with small versions of all the rides and numerous other entertainments to boot. When the Depression hit, Strehlow was unable to recoup his investment. It might have been different—Neptune, with its characteristic sparkle, might have sprung back, if not for the simultaneous completion of the Bay Bridge in 1936 and the rise of car culture that accompanied it. Neptune Beach's attractions suddenly became too close, too quaint, compared with the allure of wilder destinations—Yosemite, Lake Tahoe, Hollywood. These attractions represented a new set of Chinese jackets to catch the eye of San Franciscans looking for fun, but unlike Neptune's embroidered silk, they were within grasp.

Young people started figuring out ways to sneak into the pools for free via the bay side of the park. Admission at the front end was free already, because no one could afford it. In 1939, the city council and the Strehlow family decided to close down the park—and

it all came apart in a flash, the buildings either demolished, dismantled, or auctioned off, all for a mere fraction of what they had been worth. Wooden swans and carousel creatures were disassembled and sold to the highest bidder, their magic gone.

Now, the bayfront at Alameda's West End is a regional park, and there, a quieter, more subtle sort of splendor reigns supreme—the light of the sun on small waves; the calling of geese as they land together; the smell of salt and wind. That whirling whiplash roller coaster, those enormous pools with their fountains and lights, the beaches packed with sunbathing bodies—all now a dream that falls through the fingers like water at dawn.

Women posing in high style for a swimsuit contest circa 1917 or 1918. Courtesy of Chuck Millar

Top: An elaborate truck-drawn float advertising the extravaganzas of Neptune Beach.

Bottom left: A family photograph taken in the photo studio at Neptune Beach.

Bottom right: A group of women dressed in the latest fashion—fur coats on the beach!

All photographs circa 1917 and courtesy of Chuck Millar

A man and boys gathering prunes circa 1930. Courtesy of the California Historical Society

Fruit Orchards of the Santa Clara Valley

A perfectly ripe, rose-freckled apricot picked right off the tree at midsummer is its own small paradise. Each apricot has its own hour of ripeness, its own afternoon of perfection. One branch, heavy with fruit, will ripen at a different rate than its neighbor, due to the precise amount of sun and clear spring heat that has touched it over the many weeks since blossoming. On that branch, the apricots know their moment, and will release themselves softly into your hands when they are ready. And the perfume under those fruit-laden branches: it is sweet and rich, the smell of early summer.

Every June for almost seventy years, from the 1880s through the end of World War II, the Santa Clara Valley was heady with the plump bodies of apricots. The hundreds of orchards that covered the fertile flatland from bay to hills hummed with the sudden influx of seasonal workers come to help with the brief but astonishingly abundant apricot harvest. Apricots enjoy a very short season of fruit, a mere moon or so of heavy branches and that intoxicating smell of vanilla perfume. In Egypt, where springtime is famous for the beautiful blooms of the apricot trees, there is an old saying, "tomorrow, when there are apricots,"

which means something like "don't hold your breath," because the fruits take so long to ripen, and when they do it is for so brief a time. But as another Middle Eastern saying goes, "the only thing better is an apricot in Damascus," meaning "it doesn't get better than this." The wait is worth it.

When harvesttime came in the valley, each fruit was handpicked. Apricots bruise too easily to be shaken from the tree, and because they each ripen to their own rhythm, their harvest can't be mechanized; real human hands have to touch them—eyes and nose take in their color and scent—in order to get them at just the right moment of sweetness. For canning and jam making they were harvested a little bit early, at the yellow and one-spot-of-rose stage; for dried fruit, which comprised

up to 75 percent of the valley's production, they were gathered at the peak of their sweetness. And of course fresh apricots for the local markets—that pure glory of a sun-hot apricot—were best picked just blushing with red freckles, but not too soft. For a few sultry weeks, the valley simmered with the scent of their nectar. Kids just home from school and farmers who did not grow apricots spent June halving the harvested fruit, popping out the pits, laying them on trays. It was a sticky job, and tedious, but time to catch up or gossip (if the foreman allowed it). Children learned how to curse in several languages on the job, including Italian and Croatian, much to the chagrin of their parents.

Once full of beautiful half-moon fruits, the trays were loaded onto little wooden trolleys that were

The Santa Clara Valley in robes of white blossom, taken by Southern Pacific Photo. Courtesy of the California Historical Society

A two-horse team plowing furrows between orchard rows circa 1930. Courtesy of the California Historical Society

pushed across the farms on tracks to the sulfur kilns, where they were smoked overnight. (This somewhat dubious practice kept the apricots a beautiful orange color when they dried; otherwise they went black.) After that, the trays were laid out on the open hills for several days to dry. This wasn't without risk; every once in a blue moon it rained during the dry season. But in general, the climate of the Santa Clara Valley was perfect for sun-dried fruit; this was the first commercial sun-dried fruit operation in the modern world.

The valley was the perfect place to grow all kinds of fruit, not only apricots but also French prunes, peaches, cherries, and pears. Apricots and prunes were neck and neck as highest yield—some 2.8 million and 2.2 million pounds, respectively, were grown in 1894, and shipped all over the country by train. And the numbers only increased. The alluvial plain that comprised the valley—with the Santa Cruz mountains to the west and the Diablo range to the east— was one of the richest, sweetest, and gentlest growing environments anywhere in the world,

with long, dry summers that rarely turned to baking. The deep, rich loam of the valley had been gathering for thousands of years: rain washed soil down from the mountains, and the Guadalupe River flooded annually, suffusing the earth with silt. The dirt was gold, the climate divine. "The air [...] has a clearness and brilliance from its aridity which makes each day of the long growing season more than a day in other climates," effuses Edward Wickson in his 1912 book *The California Fruits and How to Grow Them*. It was in fact possible, some said, to see all the way to the snow-capped Sierra from the eastern ridges on a very clear day.

A postcard of apricots drying in the Santa Clara Valley. Courtesy of the California Historical Society

Prunes drying in the sun at the Home Drying Grounds in the Santa Clara Valley. Courtesy of the California Historical Society

Visitors admiring the blossoms in a prune orchard.

Opposite page, left: A postcard of Santa Clara fruit trees in full blossom.

Opposite page, right: "The Valley of Heart's Delight" was a white blanket of blossoms come spring.

All images courtesy of the California Historical Society

The first orchard trees to flourish in the valley were cultivated by mission priests, producing bountiful baskets of fruit. After them came enterprising gold rush Europeans eager to set up nurseries and graft varieties of apricot and prune. It was they, and Americans wanting to settle down rather than pan gold, who discovered the valley's deep groundwater aquifers, digging deeper for them than the Californios had done with their wells. Here was what seemed an unending spring, sweet and filtered by the earth, and they tapped it greedily. When brought up to the surface, it opened the valley to large-scale agriculture.

While the water lasted, the Santa Clara Valley was blanketed in blossoms, in plump fruit, in tray after tray of drying apricots and prunes, each one of the many farms family-run. For seventy years, this was one of the most important apricot and prune producing regions not just in the country, but in the world, exporting the majority of its dried fruit to Europe. There were thirty canneries in the valley between 1900 and 1950, where thousands of men and women worked at peach-slicing machines, at the syrup vat, or in the canning room, the conveyor belts squeaking maddeningly when they hadn't been oiled. Los Altos, Los Gatos, Santa Clara, Sunnyvale, Los Altos Hills, Cupertino, Mountain View, Gilroy, Morgan Hill, Saratoga, Campbell, San Jose— they were all orchard towns, marked by the bloom and the fruit of the trees. The Valley of Heart's Delight, the name of a local cannery, was quickly adopted as a loving epithet for the whole expanse of that prodigiously fertile and flat old floodplain.

FRUIT ORCHARD, CALIFORNIA.　　C-1069

BLOSSOM TIME IN "THE VALLEY OF HEART'S DELIGHT," SANTA CLARA COUNTY, CALIFORNIA　　600

© San Jose Chamber of Commerce

NET WEIGHT 25 LBS.

Sunsweet
CALIFORNIA'S
NATURE-FLAVORED

APRICOTS

PREPARED WITH SULPHUR DIOXIDE

GROWN AND PACKED BY

CALIFORNIA PRUNE AND APRICOT GROWERS INC.
MAIN OFFICE : SAN JOSE, CALIFORNIA.

Apricot label. Courtesy of History San José

Opposite page: A dirt road rambling through fruit groves in the Santa Clara Valley, taken by Putnam & Valentine Photo. Courtesy of the California Historical Society

In his 1922 *History of Santa Clara County California,* Eugene Sawyer wrote that "to wander among the great orchards in summer, when every tree is bending beneath its weight of fruit—purple prunes, golden apricots, and yellow peaches tinted with the crimson hues of wine—is to walk in a terrestrial paradise." Surely springtime was its own Eden too, when from the hilltops the valley was a soft blur of blossoms— the pale cream of apricots, the hummingbird-pink of peaches, the lilac-blush of prunes. Urbanites took the train down from San Francisco in spring just to picnic among the petal-carpeted orchards (and, according to disgruntled and hardworking farmers, left their litter there as evidence).

Heavenly as it looked, and smelled, and tasted, life on a fruit-tree farm was not all peaches and soft summer nights. This was hard work, a labor of love. Every season of the year, and every crop, from cherries to apricots to prunes, required its own particular attention—the time for pruning, for fruit thinning, for holding frost vigils in the early spring and lighting fires (and later, oil-burning "smudge pots") in the orchards to keep the air warm if necessary. During the harvest, work didn't stop for weekends or nightfall; you worked until the job was done. But at the end of a long day, the taste of fresh apricots—the ones just a little too bruised, or a little too ripe, for commerce—was all the sweeter, the ice creams and jams whipped up by weary but grateful hands all the more precious. As Yvonne Jacobsen, the daughter of one such orchardist, wrote, "There was hardly a farmer who worked the long hours, the punishing routine, from day to day, from month to month, from year to year, who did not grow old looking something like the crooked branches of the trees." It was a fresh-air life, devoted to trees and buds and roots, a life full of the immediacy of nature's beauty—the spring blossoms, the astonishing abundance of a summer yield, a red-tailed hawk circling the trees during lunch break, the weight of so much fruit carried in crates in men's arms.

The flourishing of apricots in the valley was a brief Eden. Like all Edens, the legacy of the fruit orchards was not without its ecological cost. Trees were sprayed with early oil-based pesticides to fend off insect and fungal diseases, and the rich marsh habitats of countless geese and ducks were decimated. The aquifers became so depleted, the water table so damaged, that the ground sank by ten feet in some places. The earth would never be able to hold as much water as it once could. Nor was that Eden without its social consequences. The Valley of Heart's Delight was not a delight to all workers, especially as the century wore on and the demands of the international market became more acute. By the sixties, terrible working conditions for Latin American fruit pickers in the South Bay had given rise to Cesar Chavez's United Farm Workers of America and a revolution in labor practices.

Meanwhile, during the postwar population boom of the fifties and sixties, the Santa Clara Valley was consumed by condominiums, shopping malls, and suburban sprawl with dizzying speed. In the face of so much development, a changing market, and the continuing globalization of agriculture, the valley's orchards vanished one by one like blossoms snapped out by frost. Such rapid suburban development, and the concretization of almost every last bit of marsh and field, has done far worse for the ducks, geese, and waters of the valley than the blooming apricots ever could.

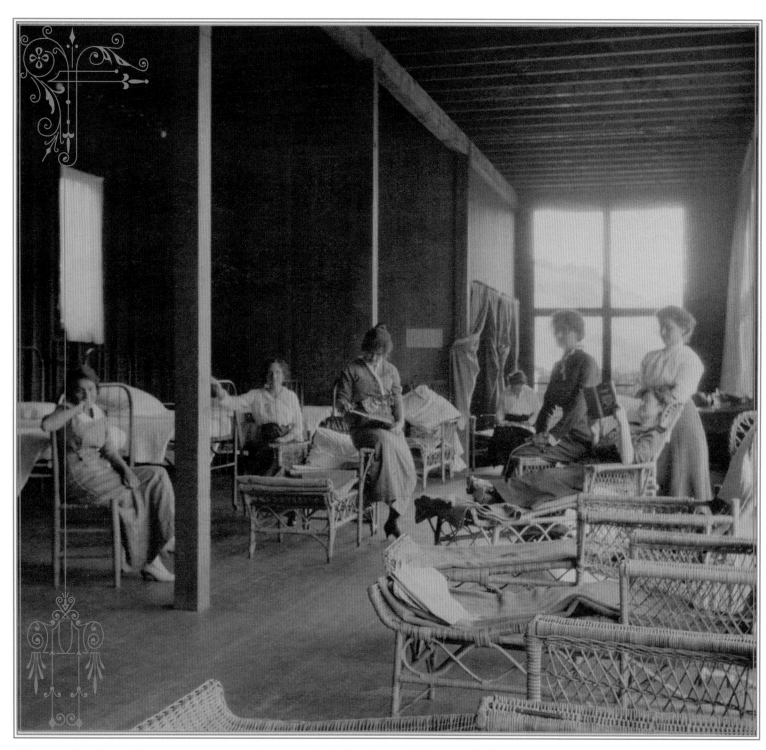

Women gathered in an infirmary room at Arequipa Sanatorium in Fairfax. Courtesy of The Bancroft Library

Arequipa Pottery

The vase is glazed the pale green of lichen, the word Madronia carved around the rim. Below the letters is a twig of madrone etched in relief, the flowers a dozen tiny cups of light. The clay holds the fingerprints of an unknown woman a hundred years gone, a woman who sat on the porch of the pottery studio at Arequipa Sanatorium in rural Fairfax, looking out across the sloping hills of bay and oak and madrone trees, lost in thought over her hand-thrown vase. Hers are daydreams that we will never catch more than a glimpse of: madrone leaf, blossom, stem. To this day, the madrones turn the curves of the hilltops above the old sanatorium red with their winter berries and white with their lantern-shaped blossoms. The blooms are so full of nectar that standing beneath a tree in the height of spring is to step into a room of honeyed beeswax candles, the bees themselves everywhere, turning the air to one sweet vibration of wings. Perhaps the maker of the Madronia vase once stood just so, her face turned up to a thousand incandescent white flowers, her hand on the cool, peeling orange bark, breathing as much sweet perfume into her lungs as she could, giving thanks for the quiet of this place, and a prayer for the slow but steady healing

Arequipa vases, featuring their signature, relief-etched flowers, inspired by specimens from the local hills. Courtesy of The Bancroft Library

of her lungs. And then, perhaps casting about later for inspiration in the pottery studio, she carved the form of the madrone into the clay.

We will never know for certain. For each vase and pot made by the tuberculosis patients at the Arequipa Sanatorium there are untold numbers of daydreams, hopes, and terrible fears captured in the curves and shadows of the clay the women shaped. There are hundreds of names on old patient records, some of whom survived and some of whom died, their lungs dark wings, and to read them out loud is to invoke a litany: Rose Linhart, Juanita Russ, Maude Nugent, Mildred Goodwin, Kume Harguchi, Julia Larson, Marcedis Truman, Violet Malik, Olga Jurlin, Edna Moore, Masa Yuasa, Adeline Firenze, Anita Eberwein. Each name a life and a mystery, but also feet that padded down the halls of Arequipa in wool socks and white nightdress at dawn, eager to catch sight of the sun turning the hills amber, or the first robins singing, or the milk truck and its handsome driver.

Though their quiet ruminations over clay are mysteries kept forever hidden inside vase and glaze, we do know that through the peace and pleasure and positive distraction of such handwork, many of these women were healed. This was Dr. Philip King Brown's original hope for the Arequipa Sanatorium, named after a small Peruvian village whose name means "place of rest" in the local indigenous language—to create a place where handcraft was central to the healing process. After the 1906 earthquake and fire, Dr. Brown had noticed that working-class women from San Francisco suffered disproportionally from the subsequent tuberculosis outbreak. Unlike their male counterparts, women generally worked in close quarters indoors as dressmakers, schoolteachers, typists and clerks, without the benefit of fresh air. In addition, when they came home they often had a husband and a house full of children to take care of, so the most important recuperative measure for early tuberculosis—bed rest—was virtually impossible for them.

In the ceramics workshop, women work on their pottery with devoted attention.

Inset: The workshop exterior, with broad windows and expansive views.

Both photographs courtesy of The Bancroft Library

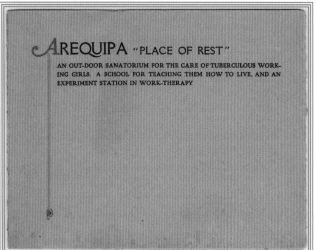

A product of the Progressive Era as well as the burgeoning Arts and Crafts movement, Dr. Brown dreamed up Arequipa, a sanatorium for working-class women with early-stage tuberculosis that, in its first decade, used pottery as a tool for healing. He hoped that women would find working with clay soothing, the creative outlet it provided uplifting, and that earning a wage through the sale of the pots would ease the feeling of being a charity case. Over the nine years of its existence, from 1911 to 1920, Arequipa Sanatorium's pottery works flourished, and so did the women who took part. At the sanatorium, patients were taught how to monitor the disease and take care of themselves, in the hopes that back at home they could avoid relapse. All expenses were covered either by wealthy philanthropists with whom Dr. Brown was connected, or by the women's employers, convinced by the doctor's compelling rhetoric that supporting an employee's recovery would be more cost-efficient in the long term than finding, hiring, and training a replacement.

Most nineteenth-century sanatoriums were sorrowful places, where death walked the long halls at night and crouched in the eaves. Dr. Brown worked hard to make Arequipa a place of both respite and light. He understood the dark power of morbid thinking, the pall that could hang over patients, the way weeks in bed with a hundred other sick women nearby gave the

Top: Two local boys loading pots into the kiln.

Bottom: The front cover of an informational pamphlet.

Both images courtesy of The Bancroft Library

Top left: Design sketches of a mermaid and a griffin for Arequipa ceramic tiles, painted by patients.

Top right: The Arequipa Sanatorium tucked away in the hills above Fairfax.

Bottom: A group of women working on their pottery outside in the woods.

All images courtesy of The Bancroft Library

A group of patients on a residential stair, with towels hanging to dry in the sun. Courtesy of The Bancroft Library

mind ample time to mull and steep and turn hopeless, so he took great care to avoid such an atmosphere. Shortly after the sanatorium's opening, one anonymous patient wrote a letter describing Arequipa's gentle atmosphere in detail—its pure dry air, ever-shining sun, the oaks and madrones and "the fragrant sweet perfume of the wildflowers," how the winding mountain road took you past crystal streams and views out over orchard, meadow, and gardens below; how the moon at night rose and illuminated everything in silver, how loud the birds were at dawn, how spacious and airy the rooms, how hearty and fresh the food. She wrote that she could think of no better name for the place, nor location for a sanatorium, and praised Dr. Brown as "a congenial whole-souled fellow [with] his heart in the right place." Another patient, Phoebe Sheldon, in a poem "To Arequipa," wrote that her heart would treasure the place "through all coming days," a place where the buckeyes bloomed like "altar candles," and the hills turned a "shadowed blue" at dawn.

Only those who had been fever-free for a week, with no cough, could work with clay, and then only for an hour at a time at first, until the supervising nurse deemed them stable enough to stay on longer—up to five hours a day. Local boys dug the clay from nearby hills, a hearty orange earth, and were trained to load and unload the kiln, as this work was deemed too physical for the patients.

A series of well-known ceramicists from England as well as the United States taught patients to use the potter's wheel and instructed them in decorative techniques before they were set loose to create the vases, bowls, and cups that were sold as Arequipa ware. The women worked outside in all but the worst weather, to take advantage of the healing properties of clean air and sun. The light and color in the glaze seemed suffused with California sun, or the green of eucalyptus, or the orange of poppies. "From the trees and plants on the grounds of the sanatorium all the designs used in the pottery are taken. Madrone, the live oak, the manzanita and all varying wild flowers—iris, cream cups, poppies, lupines, Indian paint brushes" reads a 1915 edition of the *San Francisco Chronicle*.

The whole endeavor was an almost immediate success. People were taken with the heartfelt, simple charm of the pieces, the sense that they had emerged wholly from the California environment, and moved by the story of the sanatorium women. The pottery was so well received that in 1915 Dr. Brown arranged a table at the Panama-Pacific International Exposition, where a former patient, Verna Ruegg, demonstrated wheel throwing. But more importantly, several of the most serious tuberculosis cases were drastically improved after a few months' work in the pottery, and a growing number of discharged patients were so enthusiastic

An Improper Subject

ON a recent Sunday afternoon at a large sanitarium devoted entirely to treating tuberculosis, a young Methodist minister was preaching to the assembled patients, nurses and doctors. In a most vivid manner he was describing the great peace, contentment and happiness to be had in the world to come. Suddenly one of the patients, a girl of about twenty years of age, burst out crying.

"What is the matter?" was the general chorus, as the rest crowded around her.

"Oh," she sobbed, "I wish he would stop talking about heaven. I am here paying eighteen dollars a week just to keep out of that place."

Top: A clipping from one of Arequipa's darkly humorous, patient-run papers.

Bottom: Glazed Arequipa vases and dishes.

Both images courtesy of The Bancroft Library

Rules and Regulations to be observed by the "Patients of "Arequipa" or "Place of Rest"

I. All glasses to be taken down 30 minutes after Nourishment. (This applies particularly to patients of Upper Ward, and if neglected, nourishment will be withdrawn for a period of days. to be determined by Medical Director)

II. Sun-baths to be graduated in duration — beginning at 5 mins. Sun-blistered backs or chests will not be treated under any circumstances. (This institution is Not for curing Blisters)

III. Do not spend longer than 10 mins. in dressing-room, unless you have something to show for it. (e.g. sore toe, red. nose etc)

IV. Do not leave light burning in day-time. in bright Sunshine. (This rule explains itself)

V. Do not throw rubbish in Wood-box. ("A time and place for everything")

VI. Do not put toilet articles on railing, as tooth-brushes, hair-brushes, shoes, or washing of any kind. This detracts from the aesthetic aspect of the place, and cultivates vulgar habits in patients.

VII. Do not drag chairs about. This practice scrapes floor, and breaks adhesions in lungs, and is altogether malicious.

VIII. Do not get up before the Bell. Should you be awake, lie still, and reflect on your advantages above the Waiting List.

IX. Do not waste paper-handkerchiefs. It is extravagance in War Time.

X. Do not do Spring Cleaning or Acrobatic Manoeuvres during Rest Hour. Control yourself.

XI. Do not boil Soap in washing Hair. Let someone else do it.

XII. Do not make a second fire. It engenders suspicions of Parties, etc.

XIII. Do not spill ink all over the floor. If you do, scrub it up again. (Peroxide will be found advantageous)

XIV. Do not sneeze in your towel, and kill the Chinaman.

XV. Keep your locker orderly. Do not have shirt-tails protruding from Drawers. It is unseemly.

Scrapbook #2. 42 A   (over)

A tongue-in-cheek set of "Rules and Regulations" written by an anonymous patient. Courtesy of The Bancroft Library

II

XVI. In marking clothes, place marks where they will catch eye of housekeeper. Marks placed in out-of-the-way corners, such as under cuffs or ruffles will rouse her ire, and subject you to a fine of $25.

XVII. Fill up your chart at least twice a day. What memory can be trusted for 24 consecutive hours?

XVIII. About Drugs — do not attempt to prescribe for yourself. This is the outcome of Self-Diagnosis, and will not be tolerated. However, should you want a certain drug, ask for the other kind — If you want Castor Oil, beg for Salts, and so on.

XIX. While being examined, cough in a becoming and lady-like manner for doctor. Should a cough not be forthcoming at the required moment, do not lose hope. "All things come to him who waits."

XX. [For New Patients] (a) Do not inflict a detailed account of your symptoms and Doctors upon old patients who have developed crabbiness from a constant repetition of this offence. A few general outlines, and striking facts will be sufficient.

(b) Place yourself humbly and gratefully under the tuition of the older patients, until they consider you capable of taking care of yourself.

(c) Do not consider yourself the most interesting patient that ever came to the Sanatorium. (This is to save future disillusioning.)

XXI. [In General] In case of doubt or emergency, use your Common Sense. If you have none, borrow some from a more fortunate neighbour. There are those who are always willing to lend.

Note. Patients who have been chasing the cure in this institution for over 18 months, or those who have come from Ireland, are Exempt from all the above rules. (Schedule V. act 12)

about their newfound craft that they secured housing nearby in order to continue working in the ceramics studio. It's not hard to see the appeal—Arequipa was an exceptionally beautiful and peaceful place, and outdoor work decorating vases and bowls was far preferable to long hours of dull work as a stenographer or factory worker.

Dr. Brown and his staff dotingly looked after patients, nudged them toward good health and plied them with hearty food. Nurses made fireside visits, and encouraged the women to keep to strict rules in order to maintain their health. Women were oft reminded of the "Arequipa Crawl"—the languid pace they were expected to maintain as they traversed the halls and grounds—to speak in a quiet voice, not whistle or sing, and never to stand if they could sit. These regulations inspired their own comedic imitations, as in one imaginary set of rules written in a neat hand by an anonymous patient—"do not put toilet articles on railing, as tooth-brushes, hair-brushes, shoes, or washing of any kind. This detracts from the aesthetic aspect of the place, and cultivates vulgar habits in patients [...] do not do Spring Cleaning or Acrobatic Maneuvers during Rest Hour. Control yourself. [...] Do not sneeze in your towel, and kill the Chinaman."

It is easy at first to imagine Arequipa as a place of solemn but luminous silence, young women pale and ethereal with the classic tubercular pallor, whispering in measured voices and moving very slowly down the wooden halls, but from these comedic rules, a patient-written and -read newspaper called *Hi Life*, and other personal letters, a very different version of Arequipa emerges. It was a place where humor and play

and quick jokes and a hardy irreverence breathed twinkling life through the sanatorium halls. Patients, many of whom were under thirty, jokingly called the place Dr. Brown's Charm School, filled as it was with blossoming debutantes, or the Arequipa University, with graduating classes and alumnae who must have looked to *Hi Life* and later sanatorium-run newspapers to keep tabs on old classmates.

Hi Life chronicled everything from nasty gossip to botany competitions and theatrical performances, its pages full of snark and sass and sisterhood. One Antoinette Pecarich was dubbed the "nightingale" by

Two patients dressed in costume for an outdoor performance of *Beauty and the Beast.* Courtesy of The Bancroft Library

Two patients dressed in costume. Courtesy of The Bancroft Library

the paper for her midnight concerts of snores. A Mrs. Jorgenson's squeaky shoes were "an incurable disease, as everything possible has been done." A note of condolence titled "Yoo Hoo Charlie" was written for Myrtle Aragona, who desperately waited for (and likely loudly bemoaned the delay of) a parcel from her beau. A caricature of "Daddy Brown," limbs flying in suit and bowler hat, suitcase flapping, a piece of half-eaten apple pie crammed into his mouth, was captioned "every Tuesday at 12:10 p.m." There were detailed reflections about a birthday celebrated in full Alice-in-Wonderland masquerade. Miss Williamson announced her botany competition, an event to see who could identify the most local flowers and trees. Condolences were sent to a girl out at the hospital for surgery, and for Louise Gaborine who'd hemorrhaged

and lost a baby, but was doing much better since her husband came to visit—"sometimes holding hands works like drugs." Circulated separately from *Hi Life,* but similar in spirit was the "Last Will and Testament of Irma (Rattlesnake) Newgard," in which Irma doled out an arm, a leg, her gift of gab, her enormous appetite, and her "bazooms," among other things, to various friends, including "To Hazel Keys my good eye, being far-sighted it spots men two miles away."

Perhaps these were merely game attempts at keeping chins up and spirits from flagging. For there were surely dark moments and very lonely quiet nights when breathing was hard and all thoughts turned to the morbid. But there was also kind company, and bright mornings full of the calls of robins fighting over the red madrone berries, and blue jays scolding the oaks, beaks full of acorn. And there were the pots and vases and bowls, places to carve a thousand unfathomable hopes. Though the pottery works were closed by 1920, due to the effects of World War I on the cost of raw materials, the pots themselves still survive, holding in their empty spaces something of the shape of each artist's spirit. Arequipa Sanatorium lived on in various forms until the 1950s, when penicillin made tuberculosis treatable at home, and the old buildings became property of the Girl Scouts. But in the hills above Fairfax, the madrones still bloom each spring in so many honeyed bells, white as the nightgowns of the girls of Arequipa.

The sunroom at Belgum, with wicker chairs for lounging and an elegant pool table. Courtesy of Chris Adams

Belgum Sanitarium

On a late summer day the pears are heavy as they hang from old, unpruned trees, and the massive thickets of blackberries gone feral are dark with fruit. Under the shade of the overgrown palms, cows rest and chew their cud. A hundred years ago, these pear trees, and their companion apple trees, as well as the silhouettes of a different lineage of cows, provided sustenance for the motley crew of residents at the now vanished Grande Vista Sanitarium, an insane asylum for the relations of wealthy Bay Area urbanites. It was commonly known as Belgum Sanitarium, after the Norwegian-American psychiatrist Dr. Hendrik Nelson Belgum, who bought the old stucco mansion from the Tewksbury family in 1914 and turned it into a strangely idyllic refuge from the increasingly urban Bay Area. It housed people who suffered from what Belgum politely called "nervous disorders," which it seems were mainly, in common parlance, drug addicts and alcoholics whose rich family members wanted to get them out of sight. To neighbors, it was "the crazy house." Turn-of-the-century psychiatry is a murky affair, and diagnosis often opaque. It is unclear what really plagued Belgum's patients, and how or if a line was drawn between drug addiction and mental

A view of the house at its peak, surrounded by plants and trees.

Inset: An informational pamphlet advertising the beauty, comfort, and appeal of the Grande Vista Sanitarium.

Both images courtesy of the El Cerrito Historical Society

illnesses such as schizophrenia. The place may have been simply a rehab center for substance abuse, or it may have been a live-in sanctuary for other kinds of sufferers. Whatever the case, it was a place of solace and solitude, with very little solid ground to stand upon in the historic record, and thus a place of some mystique as well.

Local children who snuck up the hill at dusk from town and around the edges of the sanitarium often heard eerily beautiful music on clarinet or piano or horn coming from the windows of the main house. Dr. Belgum held regular musical evenings with his patients, and he and two of his five sisters, who were often called "ethereal," joined in the dancing. One of them, Miss Ida Ruth Belgum, who taught third grade at nearby Washington School, was so lovely that many of the boys in her class were hopelessly devoted to her, doing all sorts of favors and chores for her so that they might get to stay after class with her to pound chalk out of the blackboard erasers, or be invited to visit Belgum for a glass of lemonade in one of the wicker rocking chairs under the soft shade of a palm tree. Ida, who was considered to be an artistic soul with European sensibilities by her family and friends, was later paralyzed in a car accident and lived upstairs at Belgum, where she continued to paint and to show her work in local galleries.

Local rogues who regularly went for dunks in the sanitarium's private springwater tanks in summer and raided the chicken coops, only to be chased off by a guard's shotgun loaded with rock salt, but in general Belgum was so tucked away, so wrapped up in its own idiosyncratic story, that outside visitors rarely came, and patients were free to roam the grounds.

The elegant Ida Belgum. Courtesy of Chris Adams

Everything about the Belgum Sanitarium had the ring of enchantment to it, the glint of something rare and tragic and beautiful, right out of a dark fairy tale. The land is gentle and sloping at the far northern end of Wildcat Canyon Regional Park, with beautiful views out over the bay toward San Francisco, Mount Tamalpais and Richmond. In the early 1900s, when the bay edges were still largely undeveloped, these vistas must have been transcendent. Down the hill, Wildcat Creek flooded to a raging, muddy torrent during the winter storms, thick with salmon, making the place all the more remote, a refuge stepped sideways out of time, where those considered mentally unstable were treated more like equals and the stars were as thick as the orchard's apple blossoms.

Dr. Belgum took the whole health of his patients into consideration in his treatment plans. Not only was his sanitarium located in a peaceful sanctuary of chaparral hills and oak forest, he also went to great lengths to turn the place into a veritable oasis-homestead. A pure-bred dairy, apiaries, a poultry plant, pear and apple orchards, vegetable gardens, and a private springwater system supplied the residents with the sweetest and freshest foods and beverages available. The house itself was all elegance and tranquility, with tall ceilings, paneled walls, dark mahogany furniture, enormous dining and living rooms, and great gleaming chandeliers that glinted and danced like constellations at night. A winding banister led to the top floor, where one long wing of small bedrooms for patients looked out over the hills toward the bay. The largest of the bedrooms housed Dr. Belgum himself, and others belonged to his three siblings.

Hendrik (sometimes "Heinrich" or other various spellings in archives) Belgum as a young man. Everyone called him simply "the Doctor." Courtesy of Chris Adams

Hendrik's library, where he kept, among other books, a fine copy of the *Encyclopedia of Health* from the early 1900s. Courtesy of Chris Adams

Ida's upstairs bedroom. Courtesy of Chris Adams

The living room of Belgum looking back toward the entryway with its grand wooden staircase. Hendrik kept his electric shock therapy machine behind the folding screen. Courtesy of Chris Adams

Hendrik, who loved to travel, driving Ida and her husband on some Sunday jaunt. Courtesy of Chris Adams

Over the years, Dr. Belgum became increasingly reclusive. It was said that he preferred the company of his patients, and his interactions with anyone from the outside world grew more and more distant. The sanitarium itself became more and more disheveled over time, with stacks of newspapers piled to the ceiling in the living room and an air of overgrown chaos nipping in at the edges. Then, with all the sudden violence of a folktale ending, a grass fire caught in the hills behind Belgum in 1948. The doctor fought desperately to keep the conflagration from consuming his beloved home. He succeeded, but the fight cost him his life.

The estate passed into the hands of Dr. Belgum's siblings. A few elderly patients also stayed on, though none of the remaining Belgums had any psychiatric or medical qualifications. It seems that family and patients instead lived together as friends, an unconventional undertaking to say the least. Barney, Hendrik's brother, spent most of his time roaming the hills until a leg wound turned gangrenous required amputation. After that, he spent all his time in the kitchen, and avoided taxes religiously. When he died in 1963, with accumulated debts and no heir willing to assume them, the place was abandoned.

Left: Hendrik's brother Barney Belgum, who took over management of the Belgum Sanitarium after Hendrik's death in 1929.

Right: Sisters Emma, Marie, and Christine Belgum.

Both photographs courtesy of Chris Adams

The site of Belgum Sanitarium after the buildings were destroyed by fire, with views out over Richmond and the bay.

Opposite page: All that remains of the main Grande Vista house is a stone foundation rimmed in overgrown fruit trees and weeds.

Both photographs courtesy of the East Bay Regional Park District

Fifteen years later, the East Bay Regional Park District added the land to the existing Wildcat Canyon Regional Park that surrounded it. By then, vandals had burned all the remaining buildings to the ground. Today, only a few stone foundations, the plantings of exotic palms, and herbs now tangled with blackberries at their bases, remain of the strange madhouse-Eden that, for a brief fifty years, flourished here.

Every spring, the narcissus still bloom: brief, sweet memories of cultivation and the dress hems of the Belgum sisters, sweeping past, stirring that smell of lost perfume. The ruins of the Belgum Sanitarium have kept their air of enchantment to this day, and it almost seems possible to imagine that the wayward hiker, gathering blackberries some summer dusk between the old palms and along the old carriage path, listening to the cows bellow and move into the night, might just hear a faint haunting music still lingering in the air as the lights of the city of Richmond flicker on below, one by one.

Looking up Montgomery Street toward the Montgomery Block in 1856. Photograph by G. R. Fardon. Courtesy of the California Historical Society

Bohemia at Monkey Block

Imagine it—a building of broad, square heft and stature, with brick walls a yard thick and every window laced with iron shutters, built on redwood logs that floated on the old sand and marsh of the bay. From the beginning, it floated on dreams. The foundation was sunk 22 feet into the ground by the sweat, shovels, and strength of hordes of Chinese laborers, and redwood logs salvaged from old ships were lashed into an enormous raft, 122 by 138 feet, bolted tight with iron. There was a twelve-by-twelve-foot layer of planking from old gold rush ships abandoned in the harbor a few years prior sunk in there too. This was in 1853, when San Francisco ended at the edge of Montgomery Street, and Henry Wager Halleck's Montgomery Block (also known as Halleck's Folly—for who builds such a structure on a raft?) was the tallest, stateliest building anywhere west of the Mississippi. Sculpted heads ringed the crown molding throughout the place. Light poured in the tall windows. And although everyone thought that Halleck was mad to build on marsh, on the backs of old ships, the regal Montgomery Block quickly filled up its courtyards and halls with a heady array of lawyers, scientists, engineers, and bankers all willing to pay a tidy sum for their offices.

Some of the most famous early land-dispute attorneys, working out the kinks after the United States snatched California from Mexico, housed their business here, as did speculators who struck it rich on Comstock silver. But in the late 1870s, the business center of San Francisco shifted south down Market Street, and a new era of tenants moved in, among them the famous literary and political publication the *Argonaut*.

It was through the *Argonaut* that the dreaming really began. Some two thousand writers, painters, photographers, sculptors, filmmakers, and musicians rented studios here from the 1870s until the building's demise in the 1960s. And it was the *Argonaut* that started the trend, bringing in some of San Francisco's early literary giants and the early stirrings of bohemia—Mark Twain, Ambrose Bierce, Gertrude Atherton, Ina Coolbrith, and Bret Harte, all of whom either worked or wrote for the magazine (or both). They made themselves at home within the imposing walls of Montgomery Block, taking studios on the upper floors (offices were kept on the first floor). There, up cool stone staircases and above a central open courtyard, studios were available

Far left: A portrait of the writer Gertrude Franklin Horn Atherton in 1904. Courtesy of the George Grantham Bain Collection, Library of Congress

Center left: A portrait of Ina Coolbrith, one of Monkey Block's most celebrated poetesses, taken in San Francisco at the Louis Thors studio around 1871, when she was 29 or 30. Courtesy of the Ina Coolbrith Collection, Oakland Public Library

Center right: A portrait of a young Mark Twain, taken in San Francisco in 1868 by Bradley & Rulofson. Courtesy of The Mark Twain Papers and Project

Far right: A portrait of Bret Harte circa 1878, one of Montgomery Block's earliest literary stars. Courtesy of The Bancroft Library

Opposite page: Like the *Argonaut*, the *Morning Call* newspaper kept its offices on bustling Montgomery Street, between Clay and Sacramento. Photograph circa 1880. Courtesy of the California Historical Society

for low rents. Small, high windows let in a flood of light. Indoor plumbing was still a rarity, but some of the studios had running water and little gas burners; these, of course, were the most prized and likely gathering places to share a cup of coffee or tea and talk over the latest poem or sketch.

It was Bret Harte, in his neat wool overcoats and bright neckties, who dubbed the area around Montgomery Block "Bohemia," inspired by contemporary Parisian artists espousing love, liberty, and revelry under the same name. "Bohemia has never been located geographically," he wrote, "but any clear day when the sun is going down, if you mount Telegraph Hill, you shall see its pleasant valleys and cloud-capped hills glittering in the west." Bohemia, and his weekly column, "The Bohemian," were Harte's way of instilling a sense of spiritual beauty and old romance into a city built on tall tales, violence, greed, and utter moral abandon.

Bohemia, as Bret Harte reckoned it, was the heart of San Francisco's Barbary Coast, where Montgomery Block was located, infamous for its saloons, its prostitutes, its rowdy brawls and nightly feasts of oysters and champagne, sometimes paid for entirely with bags of gold dust. And surely this too was part of the romance of Montgomery Block, dubbed Monkey Block by residents: by day its artists sketched and scribbled and sweated over their various creations, and by night they reveled, the streets bright with oil light and the sounds of horse hooves and wheels coming and going with carriage loads of laughing, loose women and the well-dressed men at their arms, smoking long, dark cigars. Beyond, the bay loomed, teeming with stars and fog, with the night voices of gulls and the splash of tide, and out the Golden Gate, the Pacific thrashed, untamed.

A signed portrait of George Sterling, famous poet of turn-of-the-century San Francisco, dubbed the King of Bohemia. Circa 1907.

Opposite page: Porter Garnett, George Sterling, and Jack London in Bohemian Grove, a favorite haunt of many of Monkey Block's early bohemian artists. Circa 1904–1907.

Both photographs courtesy of The Bancroft Library

San Francisco was freedom for its early writers, who sang loud against the stiff traditions of the East Coast. "O foolish wisdom sought in books!" wrote Ina Coolbrith, a tenant of Montgomery Block, in her poem "Longing."

O aimless fret of household tasks!
O chains that bind the hand and mind—
A fuller life my spirit asks!

For there the grand hills, summer-crowned,
Slope greenly downward to the seas;
One hour of rest upon their breast
Were worth a year of days like these.

And the western ocean breaks in thunder,
And the western stars go slowly under,
And her gaze is ever West
In the dream of her young unrest.
Her sea is a voice that calls,
And her star a voice above,
And her wind a voice on her walls—
My cool, grey city of love.

In San Francisco, the wild dreams of writers and artists had room to breathe, and it was the spirit of bohemianism birthed within the walls of Montgomery Block that cultivated such spaciousness. Political critique flourished, led by Ambrose Bierce's fierce pen. Anarchists who were part of this circle of Monkey Block bohemians, such as Emma Goldman, wrote bold denunciations of the current social order. By the 1890s and early 1900s, a younger generation of bohemians had arrived in the neighborhood, eagerly filling up Monkey Block studios with their easels and writing desks, their late nights full of tobacco smoke, sipping brandy and fervently discussing beauty, the soul, local politics, all of a breath. Poet George Sterling, mentee of the famous Ambrose Bierce and best friends with Jack London (they called each other Greek, for Sterling's good looks, and Wolf, for London's adventurous spirit), led the way. Sterling was praised by Bierce as a "poet of the skies, prophet of the suns," and by Robinson Jeffers—famous bard of the Carmel coast—as "the sweetest voice of the Iron Age," and was soon crowned both King of Bohemia and Poet Laureate of San Francisco. "The winds of the Future wait/At the iron walls of her Gate," wrote Sterling of his beloved city.

Felix Piantanida and Poppa Coppa standing at the bar in Coppa's restaurant, the famous bohemian haunt. Courtesy of the San Francisco History Center, San Francisco Public Library

Opposite page: View from the Mills Building circa 1890. Courtesy of the California Historical Society

Every crowd of bohemians of course needs its watering hole, and a place known as Coppa's played the part brilliantly. Located on the ground floor of Montgomery Block, Coppa's restaurant was elegant and smoky, touched with an old-world Italian style, and the food both delicious and well priced (Giuseppe Coppa trained as a chef in Paris). The walls were a deep red that, by 1905, were covered in murals and a so-called "Bohemian Wall of Fame," crowned by painter Xavier Martínez's stenciled black cats, a nod to Le Chat Noir in Paris. Of a cold summer evening with the fog drifting over the bay, you might find a crowd of Monkey Block artists around a back table, sipping port, smoking long cigarettes. George Sterling, with his chiseled silhouette, would be looking rakishly handsome as he brooded over a manuscript with Jack London, who might be leaning back to consider some cadence or meter, his feet propped up on the table, swilling a tumbler of whiskey. Meanwhile, Xavier Martínez might be seen painting a new figure on the wall—one of the crew, maybe Bertha Brubaker standing in a long white dress with a cigarette at her lips. Above her, and below the rim of black cats, marched the banner of names—famous writers throughout history, with local artists interspersed. Dante, Martínez, Villon. Goethe, Sterling, Nietzsche. Even in their day, the bohemians of Monkey Block were so well known, so poetic, charismatic, and mysterious, that locals thronged Coppa's, hoping for a snatch of their lively banter or a glimpse of their long coats.

Although Coppa's closed after the 1906 earthquake, it reopened under various names and managements throughout the neighborhood, most famously as the Black Cat. This scene continued around Montgomery Block—the poets, the muralists, the journalists, the photographers, all gathering over coffee or wine to feverishly discuss their dreams—until the end of the 1950s.

Generations of writers and artists followed the path laid by those first self-proclaimed Bohemians of the late 1870s who created a culture of freedom, of romance, of wildness. Many were those funded by the Federal Art Project of the 1930s, which subsidized rents at Montgomery Block to help support painters, photographers, writers, and sculptors throughout the Depression— Diego Rivera and Frida Kahlo made a brief but illustrious appearance!—and after them the Beat poets, from Jack Kerouac and Allen Ginsberg to Lawrence Ferlinghetti. The spirit of anarchy, of countercultural radicalism, had been present from the beginning among the pens of Twain and Harte, Sterling and Coolbrith, in the narrow light-filled studios of Montgomery Block and at the rowdy, smoke-ringed tables of Coppa's.

By the time Monkey Block was knocked down in 1959 to build a parking lot, which was followed by the Transamerica Pyramid in 1972, it had sheltered almost a hundred years of artists, Bohemians to Beats. Its transformation from a place of dreams that floated on underground logs at the edge of the city, to a skyscraper full of corporate bankers, was bittersweet at best.

The poets have fled elsewhere, now, to dream.

A group standing at Montgomery Block's entrance in 1938, when it was home to some of the city's most talented artists during the Great Depression. Courtesy of the San Francisco History Center, San Francisco Public Library

Montgomery Block between Clay and Washington in 1880. Courtesy of the California Historical Society

An old cable car being hoisted to the roof of the Emporium in 1948, to be placed in the roof garden as a "memoriam to early days of California," as the *San Francisco Call-Bulletin* reported. Courtesy of the San Francisco History Center, San Francisco Public Library

The Emporium Department Store

Ten thousand white lights blaze overhead. The rotunda dome floods sun through 140 feet of delicately wrought metal and glass down upon a central bandstand, café, and marble-floored atrium. The warm smells of fresh tea-sandwiches and new leather shoes, the bright Oriental rugs, and busy shoppers flushed with excitement. The place is a hive, fifteen elevators in all to connect the mezzanines, each floor stuffed with fancies to catch the eye, from china to curtains. The cash boys dashing to and fro, feet slapping the marble floors between customer and cashier with change. Later, in their place, an elaborate system of pneumatic tubes rippling throughout each department like roots, brass cylinders zooming every which way, moved by air pressure up to the cash office and back down again to the requisite seller, full of change and a receipt. Imagine! The noise, the lights, the palatial space teeming with shoppers both well heeled and modest, the state-of-the-art technology, those little brass tubes flying like wishes from room to room. In the middle of it all, ringed by a café-restaurant, was the bandstand, raised up on a platform like some gilded mushroom, where full orchestral arrangements were performed three times a week.

The place must have been dazzling. Its whole purpose, in fact, was just that—to dazzle, to bewitch, to overwhelm the senses, to draw you in so that you could not help but leave with some bright new treasure, packed carefully in tissue and tied up with string. Soft leather gloves. A new watch. Silverware. A bit of candy. A new set of chairs for the dining room. Though the Emporium was a center of commerce, it was also a gathering place, a new kind of community hub in a quickly changing urban world. A visit warranted putting on your best clothes, for it meant heading downtown to that place of astonishing light and loft, that great tiered hall of many chiming voices and teaspoons clattering against cups and violins lilting out from the bandstand. Immediately, smooth-talking, well-groomed attendants ("floorwalkers") were at your elbow, steering you toward just the right pair of shoes, the perfect set of pots and pans, the most economical linens, the best place for a young boy to get a haircut. Or, alternatively, toward a "silence room" if your nerves were in need of a bit of peace and quiet, or to a dark room lit with gaslight to imitate a ballroom, where women could try on ball gowns in the proper lighting. The Emporium was also a place to spend the day—to meet a friend for tea, to post a letter and have lunch and listen to a concert. There was nowhere else to go in the city that offered a similar combination of necessity and indulgence, nowhere else that so automatically invited anyone and everyone into elegance.

The Emporium was not San Francisco's first department store, but it was its most popular and longest-lasting, opening its doors in 1896 and closing them at last in 1995. For the first half of its life in particular it was a community establishment where women met for tea and stayed all afternoon to listen to a concert while their children were looked after in the nursery. It was where little boys were taken to buy their first grown-up jacket or to meet Santa Claus at Christmas under the enormous yuletide tree gleaming with lights. The Emporium cut a regal figure along the south side of Market Street, with its seven-story Beaux-Arts façade. Designed by architect Albert Pissis in the spirit of the arcades of London and Paris, with marble mosaic along the front sidewalk, the *San Francisco Chronicle*

The exterior of the Emporium from busy Market Street circa 1904. Courtesy of the San Francisco History Center, San Francisco Public Library

Opposite page: A window display featuring the latest fashions circa 1909. Courtesy of the California Historical Society

The brightly lit corridors of the Emporium in 1915.

Inset: A postcard from one of the Emporium's cafés.

Both photographs courtesy of the California Historical Society

compared it to Pompeii in 1896, and called it "the finest store in all the world."

On the broad street outside—the city's widest in its early years, cutting a broad swath straight through from the waterfront to Twin Peaks—horses and buggies, and later cable cars, rushed to and fro, bringing customers from all over the city, and from the ferry that docked regularly at the Embarcadero with visitors from Oakland and beyond. The Emporium took up most of the block, and though it wasn't on the fashionable side of the street near Union Square, where earlier, more aristocratic department stores like the City of Paris and the White House were located, it quickly won hearts and allegiances, never intending to cater to the rich alone. The Emporium advertised itself as a store for everyone and everything, and succeeded royally as such. An 1897 newspaper advertisement boasted that "the 60-odd departments carr[ied] the best of everything to eat, drink, wear or use in your homes." Headlines advertised genuine bargains in shoes, fall dress goods and silks, hosiery and knit underwear, suits and cloaks, rubber goods, wines and liquors, men's hats, furniture and carpets, stationery, venetian laces, curtains and curtain nets, the best French mixed candy; furthermore, it was said to be a place "for book lovers." It was a far cry from the country store where most of the

Top: The Emporium dome and rotunda, showing the main aisle through the grandstand in 1905. Courtesy of the San Francisco History Center, San Francisco Public Library

Bottom: The band stand and café in the center of the Emporium. Courtesy of the California Historical Society

population (save the very wealthy) was accustomed to shopping, a place where vegetables were sold alongside dry goods (fabric, petticoats, underpants) and sundries (cologne, tooth powder, razors), the whole affair packed into a modest storefront. Here, in the newfangled department stores of the late 1800s, luxury items normally reserved for upper-class establishments competed for space with sacks of flour; women's makeup was thrillingly displayed on cosmetic counters for all to see; and you could stop for a meal

The fabric display in the Emporium Department Store circa 1915.
Courtesy of the California Historical Society

while you browsed—the first seeds of our culture of consumption, which transformed shopping from a chore into a pleasurable pastime, were planted.

Department stores rose to prominence in Europe and the United States in the second half of the nineteenth century, the product of the industrial revolution, a burgeoning middle class, and the sudden growth of cities and urban centers. The industrial revolution changed the whole social landscape—people flocked to cities, labor was cheap and goods suddenly plentiful. With that sudden ease came a higher standard of living, and wage earners with more money to spend were eager to spend it somewhere, eager to get in on the new comforts of their new middle-class lifestyle. Department stores rushed in to meet the demand, providing a wide variety of elegant commodities on the

cheap, while cultivating the need for said commodities at the same time. San Francisco, which from the beginning had tumbled gold-dust luxury and gritty frontier life together, took to the concept wholeheartedly.

Early department stores were the pioneering advertisers; they learned how to sell more than just the thing itself—to sell an experience, a lifestyle all tied up with string. At the Emporium, a young woman might buy her own little piece of classy femininity in the shape of a fine pair of gloves, or a man might purchase what advertising told him was a marker of masculine success: an exquisite pair of Italian leather shoes. More problematic trends found a foothold too, such as an early-twentieth-century craze for California Indian basketry. Beautiful baskets woven by native women were fetishized in women's magazines and sold like hotcakes. They were coveted as parlor pieces, reflections of a romantic but dying way of life, even as this very attitude of objectification was rapidly destroying the traditional ways it sought to glamorize. Advertising told the stories that sold best, and for a place like the Emporium, an exotic Indian "basket craze" only added to the allure of its shelves.

From the early days, the Emporium inspired loyalty. When the 1906 earthquake and fire nearly leveled the building, destroying not just goods but detailed customer accounts, one of the reasons the store didn't go under immediately was the honesty of its customers, most of whom hurried to the makeshift new location behind a private house on Polk and Van Ness and paid

A crowd gathered on Eddy Street on April 18, 1906, to watch in horror as the Emporium burned after the earthquake.

Inset: In the end, the front façade was all that remained of the Emporium after the 1906 earthquake.

Both photographs courtesy of the San Francisco History Center, San Francisco Public Library

People gathered outside the front door of the ruined Emporium after the 1906 earthquake.

Opposite page: Wreckage inside the Emporium caused by the 1906 earthquake and fire.

Both photographs courtesy of the San Francisco History Center, San Francisco Public Library

Workmen guiding a new merry-go-round horse up to the roof of the Emporium in 1957, as they prepare for the opening of the Emporium roof rides. Courtesy of the San Francisco History Center, San Francisco Public Library

A crowd of people wait to ride the new escalator at the Emporium circa 1936. Courtesy of the San Francisco History Center, San Francisco Public Library

up their accounts, knowing full well that evidence of their debts had been lost. The rebuilt Emporium—façade still miraculously intact—was more popular than ever when it reopened in 1908, becoming a veritable San Francisco institution. By the 1940s, the Emporium's wintertime display was a destination in itself, not only the enormous Christmas tree decorated with bright lights and the red-velvet Santa ready to hear the Christmas wishes of a long line of children, but most important, the seasonal holiday roof rides.

The elevator ride up through the rotunda dome and onto the rooftop was reminiscent of the glass elevator in Willy Wonka's Chocolate Factory, breaking through a ceiling and into the sky. In this case, the elevator opened onto a small menagerie of rooftop rides that grew steadily in number each year. A Ferris wheel, roto cars, the Little Dipper roller coaster, a merry-go-round, not to mention cotton candy and popcorn stands. Imagine it, being a little child in your best coat and hat at the peak of that Ferris wheel, belly full of some sugary treat, swinging up over the whole of San Francisco and able to take in its hills and straight-line streets, the new red Golden Gate Bridge, the thick blue of the bay, the winter-clear sky in one glorious instant. What brief, what effervescent delight. On the elevator afterward, down all seven floors with hands and nose numb and red, past the great tree and out through the hum of the place: a labyrinth of shoes and chairs and tea sets and fancy new appliances and bedsheets and candies and reels of lace in that open, marble-bright arcade. Out on the street in the fresh air, all dizzy and dazzled, the place must have seemed a strange sort of dream, the kind to tuck away in your pocket beside the new bag of Danish rhubarb candies, until next time.

After World War II, as the population of the Bay Area increased dramatically, the Emporium became a chain enterprise, expanding into suburban neighborhoods from San Mateo to Marin. And in that transformation, something vital was lost. The mechanization and commodification of the world was in full tilt. Brand names began to take on a new meaning, to gain a new, homogenizing kind of power. By the time the Emporium at last closed its doors under that name in 1995, it had been bought and sold many times by the likes of Macy's and others. It is now the Westfield San Francisco Centre, and packed with chain stores. It is no longer comprised of so many unique parts, no longer a patchwork, grown up from the soil of San Francisco, with tea and orchestral music and the sense that you were in on something special, something one-of-a-kind, with its own traditions and stories. Now, a department store is a glorified shopping mall, and the world is overrun with cheap commodities pedaled to us with all of their true costs hidden behind glitzy exteriors. Perhaps it was always this way. The Emporium was surely the beginning. And yet in its beginnings were the colors and attitudes of an older world, which have all but faded from view.

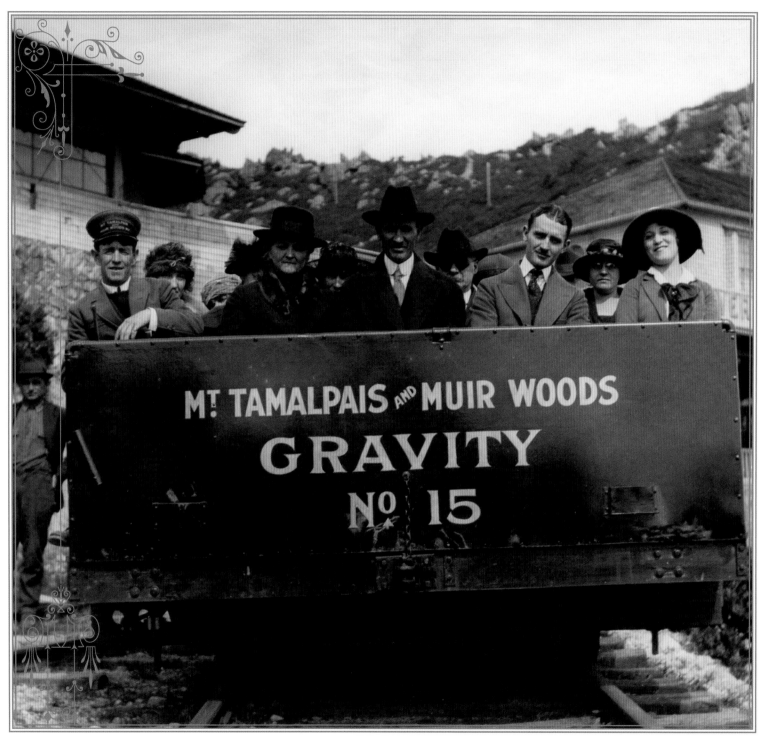

A gravity car full of passengers at the Tavern, readying for descent circa 1915. Courtesy of the Mill Valley Public Library History Room

The Mount Tamalpais and Muir Woods Railway

Riding the sturdy, fresh-painted steam train as it wound up and up to the peak of Mount Tamalpais was an occasion for your Sunday best. When you arrived, the Tavern, perched there at the top of the world and looking out over ocean, hills, bay, and city, was full of visitors, good food, and champagne. And on the ride back down, through Muir Woods in the gravity car, the wind was sweet and full of bay and redwood spice. Such a journey was a cause for celebration, something to be greeted in a fine hat and shoes. It became almost a duty to take visitors, especially important ones, for a day trip up to the top of the beautiful bay mountain so that they could be thoroughly dazzled and awed. Governors from around the country, visiting royalty, famous writers and artists—all went up to the peak to be staggered by that span of beauty. From San Francisco's early days, Mount Tamalpais—rising steep just north of the Golden Gate right up out of ocean and bay—was much beloved and much boasted of, the favorite destination for weekend hiking trips and Sunday picnics. Its peak, at 2,571 feet, was the highest in the area, bested only by Mount Diablo about thirty miles east of the bay.

Before the mountain railroad, adventurers craving such heights left the city early by ferry, then caught a leg of the North Pacific Coast Railroad to Mill Valley and set off through the foothills, tramping up steep canyons of madrone and live oak, redwood and fern, manzanita and a good measure of tawny dust, to reach the east peak. It was an all-day affair, a summer's dawn to dusk, with weary legs and sore feet by nightfall. But it was well worth the exertion—to feel each new ridge and hillside and forest path underfoot, to picnic in any inviting meadow rimmed with moss-hung firs, to wade through poppies and baby blue eyes in early spring, to stand, breathless, as fog from the ocean suddenly breached the ridge up ahead and began to billow downhill like smoke, turning the world to a tingle of mist. What total peace, what silence, was there to be found, a peace and silence that were to be completely transformed by the arrival of the steam trains.

There were those who did not welcome the opening of the Mill Valley and Mount Tamalpais Scenic Railway in 1896, walkers who feared the loss of their mountain solace, the inevitable crowds and smoke and noise. And there were residents back in Mill Valley's Corte Madera canyon who protested the construction of train tracks right outside their homes so vociferously that lawyers and law enforcement had to be brought in. Even then, one Mrs. McInnes managed to overturn a six-team plow that was preparing to dig the roadway outside her house. Despite some local resistance, the inaugural run of the steam train in August 1896 was met with great enthusiasm, much toasting of champagne, and copious glowing reviews written by the local press, who called it "the grandest day's outing in the world." Local trampers found that catching a steam train from downtown Mill Valley up to the Tavern on the peak, enjoying a meal, and then hiking back

Tavern on Mount Tamalpais circa 1905.
Courtesy of the California Historical Society

A locomotive pulling a gravity car near the summit of Mount Tamalpais circa 1922. Courtesy of the California Historical Society

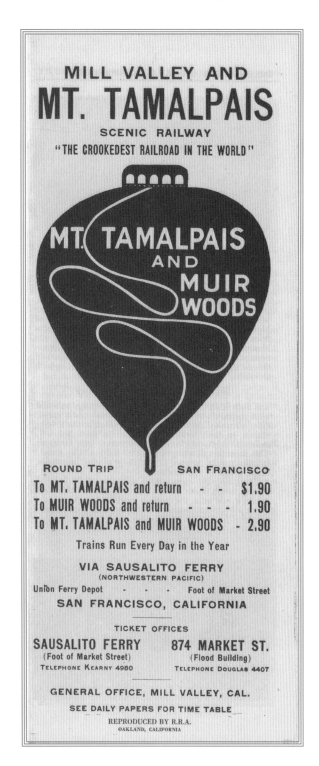

MILL VALLEY AND

MT. TAMALPAIS

SCENIC RAILWAY
"THE CROOKEDEST RAILROAD IN THE WORLD"

MT. TAMALPAIS
AND
MUIR WOODS

ROUND TRIP   SAN FRANCISCO

To MT. TAMALPAIS and return - - $1.90
To MUIR WOODS and return - - - 1.90
To MT. TAMALPAIS and MUIR WOODS - 2.90

Trains Run Every Day in the Year

VIA SAUSALITO FERRY
(NORTHWESTERN PACIFIC)
Union Ferry Depot - - -   Foot of Market Street
SAN FRANCISCO, CALIFORNIA

TICKET OFFICES

SAUSALITO FERRY   874 MARKET ST.
(Foot of Market Street)   (Flood Building)
TELEPHONE KEARNY 4980   TELEPHONE DOUGLAS 4407

GENERAL OFFICE, MILL VALLEY, CAL.

SEE DAILY PAPERS FOR TIME TABLE

REPRODUCED BY R.R.A.
OAKLAND, CALIFORNIA

down through redwood and bay was also a delightful way to spend a Sunday, and even John Muir himself, lover of pristine wilderness, called the Mount Tamalpais Railway a "delightful ride." By 1907, the railroad extended through Muir Woods, so that a day's adventure might include a morning ride up to the peak of the mountain, lunch at the Tavern, a gravity car down through the giant redwoods, and another train back to Mill Valley, in time for the evening ferry back to Market Street. Gravity cars, introduced in 1902, became a fast favorite—little four-wheeled carriages that coasted down the mountain's steep grade from the summit all the way to Muir Woods. And the West Point Inn, built in 1904 and originally little more than a way station where stagecoach riders coming up from Stinson Beach (then called Willow Camp) could transfer to the train, quickly became its own overnight destination. A more romantic location for a pint of ale and a meal by firelight can hardly be imagined—not with those views of steep, redwood-thick hills, the ocean a blue-gray quilt beyond, the fog sometimes its own landscape, rolling in, the absolute silence of the darkness, save the whistle and huff of the train.

The Muir Inn at Muir Woods, National Park, Mt. Tamalpais, Marin County, California.

The railroad tracks that clung to the steep slope of Mount Tamalpais curved 281 times so trains could safely make the ascent. This gave passengers 281 opportunities to exclaim in delight when a sudden vista of the bay and its islands, or the headlands and ocean beyond, emerged through the trees. One of the most famous stretches of track was called the Double Bow Knot. Four curves in all, the train tracks switch-backing five times to gain the next leg of elevation, the Double Bow Knot looked down over ridges of man-zanita and coyote brush all the way to the bay. At the top, passengers could transfer to the Muir Woods grav-ity car and coast back down to the cool, damp shade of ancient trees. The gravity car route was often called the "world's longest roller coaster," but its conductor, called the "gravityman," was known to soothe nervous passengers, reminding them that the train never went above twelve miles per hour, save at a single stretch of level track near Fern Canyon to keep up momentum. Coasting down the whole mountain at that gentle pace, canyons and forests rolling past silent and soft, must have been deeply peaceful, the wind fresh on your face, the din of the city far, far away. Moonlit rides down were especially popular—the moon flashing through the trees, turning streams to silver, the world dappled. Extra trains ran up and down the mountain on days of full moon and eclipse, as well as the more stan-dard celebrations such as New Year's Eve, Christmas, Thanksgiving, and, after 1913, for Mountain Plays in summertime at the outdoor amphitheater above Pan-toll Station.

A gravity car and its driver near the summit circa 1909.
Courtesy of the Mill Valley Public Library History Room

Opposite page, left: A pamphlet advertising the world's "crookedest railroad," with fares and attractions. Courtesy of the Mill Valley Public Library History Room

Opposite page, right: The Muir Inn at Muir Woods National Park.
Courtesy of the California Historical Society

There were of course the inevitable dangers, the ones that came from the wild land itself. Sometimes, great gales suddenly blew in, howling against the peak of the mountain with such force that Tavern visitors grew afraid the whole place would be torn away in a gust; now and then they had to be evacuated by rail down to lower ground. This meant that the train crew had to detach the engine's 150-pound headlamp and wrangle it inside to light it there, away from the wind. More serious was the risk of wildfire, already a strong possibility during the long, dry summers, made more likely by the coming and going of the trains themselves through the thick, resinous, fire-loving brush. Even though the steam engines were upgraded early on to burn oil instead of wood due to the fire risk, the heat of the wheels, tracks, and locomotives, and the inevitable flying sparks, led to several dangerous wildfires on the mountain. Visitors evacuated by train from the Tavern at the peak would fly down through stifling smoke and walls of flames, and in a 1913 fire, champagne was reportedly poured on hot metal to keep the train cool. The champagne was also given in "big draughts to the ladies who needed it as a bracer," according to Mrs. Grace Gilliland, wife of the tavern keeper. Still, on the whole, the "crookedest railroad in the world" was an elegant, beautiful ride, peaceful and exhilarating both, a "tonic for mind and body," as was written in a 1918 advertisement.

Being so winding, crooked, and steep, not to mention packed full to the brim with eager passengers (especially during the "good years" from around 1906 to 1916), you would expect at least a few accidents from the Mount Tamalpais and Muir Woods Railway.

A bird's-eye view of the Double Bow Knot and the foothills of Mount Tamalpais. Courtesy of the Mill Valley Public Library History Room

Opposite page: Sightseers near the top of the mountain gathered on a lookout rock near the terminus of the railroad. Photograph by Fred Ransome. Courtesy of the California Historical Society

A group of friends gather under the trees of Muir Woods.

Inset: One of the giant redwoods of Muir Woods.

Both images courtesy of the California Historical Society

3278-A Redwood Giant of Muir Woods
Mt Tamalpais Railway, California

A gravity car coasting down toward Muir Woods past an old moss-hung oak. Courtesy of the Mill Valley Public Library History Room

But safety measures were so thorough, and followed so strictly, that not a single passenger was killed during all thirty-four years of the railroad's existence; only two employees lost their lives; and mishaps in general were very few. Safety was mainly ensured by always keeping the locomotive engine of the train downslope of the passenger cars—so that they were in fact pushed up the mountain, and then carefully pulled back down. This way, there was no possibility of a breakaway car. Double-enforced sets of brakes, strict speed limits, and careful training for train conductors helped too. But during off hours, railway workers bent the rules a little—in the small hours of the morning, locomotive engineer and shop-man Valley Thorney supposedly made it down from the top of the mountain to Mill Valley by gravity car in twenty-one minutes. He hit a deer on the way, the poor creature transfixed by the din of the oncoming vehicle, no doubt astonished and confused by such a fast, loud, moving box breaking up the quiet of the night—a vehicle that portended the coming of many, many more, and so much the worse for the gentle deer of the mountain, frequent casualties of the roadway.

COTTAGES MUIR WOODS
MT. TAMALPAIS & MUIR WOODS RY, CALIFORNIA.

Wooden cabins near Muir Inn along the railway.
Courtesy of the California Historical Society

Scientific journals, travel columns, and train experts praised the railway as one of the most "remarkable pieces of railroad engineering in the country," and "the most charming and unique of California's gifts to the world." But no matter its romance, its ingenuity, its popularity in the early part of the twentieth century, the mountain railroad was no match for the coming of the automobile. As early as 1920, people were making a go at driving their motor trucks up the railroad ties, and by 1928 buses from the city were all the rage, quicker and easier than the various legs of train travel. A huge fire engulfed many of the railroad ties in 1929, sealing the deal, and the Mount Tamalpais and Muir Woods Railway was closed by 1930, its tracks jacked up and ties removed with sledgehammers. Several gravity cars found new homes in Mill Valley gardens, and one lives to this day in the Depot Plaza, scrambled over by generations of children.

Now, much of the mountain is quiet once more, no black billows of engine smoke streaming out against her flanks, no steam whistles echoing through her canyons, no hum and huff of locomotive engines. The route of the railroad is a broad hiking trail, a long portion of it called Old Railroad Grade in memory of the train, where walkers again make the delightful tramp up to the peak on foot to look out over the entire bay, west to the Farallones, and sometimes, on a clear day, as far as the snowcaps of the Sierra.

A crew of men clearing the railroad track in 1930, with the East Peak looming in the background. Courtesy of the Mill Valley Public Library History Room

Women picnicking on the beach beyond Carville, with the Cliff House in the distance circa 1905. Courtesy of the California Historical Society

THE SAND DUNES OF OLD SAN FRANCISCO

The dunes had always been home to hardy yellow lupines, and the pewter-blue butterflies called Xerces, whose only home in the world was the western, ocean-facing half of San Francisco. Great winds shaped the dunes like tides, moving sand in gusts so that the landscape was never the same from one day to the next. The dunes were an extension of the pounding and gale-filled seaboard, the edge of the world where land sifted into wave, only here and there touched with the speckled blue flash of a butterfly, the bronze and panting dash of a coyote, the scuttling green iridescence of a tiger beetle. When a strong wind came, it ran unimpeded—save for the low-growing lupines and deerweeds and little stunted willows along seeps and small creeks. The sand was vast in every direction like some seaside Sahara—from present-day Golden Gate Park all the way south to Lake Merced, and inland to Mount Sutro. On a dark night the winds might take your very name away for a moment in favor of cold stars and ocean and howling weather, bracing and clean as the beginning of time.

Until the early 1900s, San Francisco's expanse of dunes was called the Outside Lands, or, more simply, the Great Sand Waste, a place that most city residents

Purple lupines and dune flowers in the great sands of San Francisco. Courtesy of the California Historical Society

considered desolate, barren, and forbidding—a kind of no-man's-land. Some of the dunes were over one hundred feet high, and caught the winds that blew unhindered northwest from the San Francisco Peninsula. The sand was defiant, and did not take easily to development: always transforming, always blowing, always getting into shoes and socks and even the heaviest coats, never offering a reliable foothold for more than a few moments. Even on a still day, fine sand undulating up and down in giant dunes was difficult to navigate on foot, but such a landscape was harder still to traverse by horse and carriage. Esteban Richardson, who grew up in the 1840s, the grandson of a presidio comandante, remembered how "the wind carried with it an almost incredible burden of both fine and coarse sand that got into clothes, eyes, nose, mouth—anything that was open in short—besides penetrating the innermost recesses of a household." This was not the place for a settlement, let alone a city, but San Francisco's population explosion and staggering growth from the start of

A view of Seal Rock House looking southeast from Cliff House in 1868, with sand dunes and a future Golden Gate Park beyond. Courtesy of the San Francisco History Center, San Francisco Public Library

the gold rush through the early 1900s sealed the fate of the sand dunes, which fell slowly but inevitably to builders, first marshaling steam shovels and later electric bulldozers.

As early as 1849, attempts were already being made to flatten some of the dunes—nothing could be done about the wind—but this was difficult work and it rarely took hold. In the years before the turn of the century, many of the sand dunes stayed mostly as wild as they had been for millennia, transformed only here and there by dairy ranches, a chicken farm, four cemeteries—a wasteland was a good place to bury a growing city's dead—and Samuel Brannan's Cliff House resort in 1863. Wealthy visitors to the resort demanded the city build a road over the sand dunes to make the place easier to get to, and while the road attracted more settlers to the area, houses were built slowly, a few at a time, with wooden planks laid over the sand for access. Displacement of sand by wind only grew worse as development increased because more and more of the lupines, wind-stunted little oaks, and coyote brush that had kept the sand in place were cleared or cut down for firewood. But the conjuring of Golden Gate Park right in the middle of all that sand in the 1870s and '80s stood as proof that the shifting, blustery "wasteland" could be conquered and transformed into gardens, stands of cypress and eucalyptus, and lawns so completely convincing that the sand below was soon forgotten.

Another sandy view of the Richmond District from Fourth Avenue and Clement Street. Courtesy of the California Historical Society

The early, sandy Richmond District at the northwest corner of Point Lobos and Eighth Avenue.
Courtesy of the California Historical Society

In 1895, when the Market Street Railway Company started selling old horse-drawn street cars in favor of new electric ones, people began to move in larger numbers to the "Outside Lands." The streetcars were complete house structures already, portable and finely finished—and they sold for ten dollars apiece without the seats. The great dunescapes of the city's western frontier were largely empty—a perfect place to put your new house-on-wheels! By 1900, one hundred streetcar-houses were nestled among the sand dunes facing Ocean Beach, a motley and bohemian enclave, like some gathering of nesting seabirds. In the beginning, many of the horse-car houses were actually restaurants, beach cottages, and clubhouses on then-mayor Adolph Sutro's land, among the women's Falcon Cycling Club, and a musical gathering place called La Bohème. After the 1906 earthquake, Carville-by-the-Sea, as the community was called, became a settlement for refugees, and by the 1950s, many of the streetcars had been absorbed into more traditional apartment structures.

Early Carville houses standing in the sand and wind. Courtesy of the San Francisco History Center, San Francisco Public Library

By that time, the feats of modern engineering and sheer hubris that had transformed sand dunes into Golden Gate Park had likewise turned much of the once-"wasteland" into streets and apartment buildings that became proper city districts—the Sunset and the Richmond.

To the ravenous city, the sand dune "wasteland" was seen from the beginning as a nuisance and an impediment to progress—blowing where it shouldn't, shift-ing into the street when your back was turned, a chore to get a horse and carriage to traverse, un-pinnable, un-griddable, and worse still, notably infertile and difficult to grow any "useful" plants upon without large amounts of expensive water and manure. But the sand dunes were in truth far from barren—it just took an expert sort of eye to notice their own shy language of fecundity. From its earliest days, San Francisco attracted not only gold-seekers but also naturalists drawn to the

The interior of a house car in Carville.

Inset: An overhead peek into a Carville neighborhood.

Both photographs courtesy of the San Francisco History Center,
San Francisco Public Library

abundance of plant and animal life around the bay, an abundance that is almost unimaginable today. The city's sand dunes inspired the devotion of a number of entomologists and amateur naturalists alike, including George Dunn, who in 1892 made a minute study of San Francisco's coastal strand ecosystem. A waste, people called the dunes, but not Dunn. Burrowing in sand, nesting in lupine branches, feeding on deerweed, fifty species of beetle and mollusk, twenty-nine species of spider, and seven kinds of mite, and numerous butter-

flies and moths were documented by Dunn. In all, he recorded some 221 insect species that called the sand dunes home, attuned as he was to their jeweled and infinitesimal worlds from his many hours crouched and peering into the grains.

One particularly beautiful little gem of a creature, the Xerces blue butterfly, carried the fate of the dunes on its silver and lapis wings. By the 1870s, naturalists and entomologists were growing vocal about the loss of butterfly abundance and diversity across the

One of the old gravestones in the Laurel Hill Cemetery, later used in seawalls along Ocean Beach.
Courtesy of the California Historical Society

The Laurel Hill Cemetery in 1940, shortly before it was dug up to make way for development. Courtesy of the California Historical Society

dunescape; the Xerces blue, endemic to the coastal dune ecosystem of the San Francisco Peninsula alone, its range constrained by the reach of fog, stirred special concern. Hans Hermann Behr, a German naturalist, butterfly expert, and early member of the California Academy of Sciences, predicted that the Xerces blue would become extinct within his lifetime. Behr had already observed the decline of countless butterfly species and their habitats across the city, and he did in fact watch the Xerces completely disappear from the San Francisco dunes by 1875. He wrote to a colleague in Chicago that "the locality where it used to be found is converted into building lots, and between German chickens and Irish hogs no insect can exist besides louse and flea," but in later years naturalists managed to relocate a small population to a lonely patch of dunes above Lobos Creek, where yellow bush lupine, the Xerces' primary food, still grew.

Despite these tender efforts, by 1941, the Xerces blue was last observed at the Laurel Hill Cemetery where a few odd lupines and deerweeds grew among the graves. It was the first butterfly to vanish completely from North America. The sands of San Francisco were gone too, except for a small patch at Ocean Beach. There, they were held in—and kept out of the roads— by a fortified retaining wall made in part by old gravestones from the very same Laurel Hill Cemetery, which was dug up to make way for housing and offices in the mid-forties. Bodies were relocated to a mass grave at no cost, but families had to purchase headstones back from the cemetery within ninety days if they wanted to keep them. Most were abandoned, used instead for breakwaters at the Marina and Aquatic Park, gutters in Buena Vista Park, and the retaining wall at Ocean Beach. The names of San Francisco's dead were scattered throughout the city, epithets and surnames and dates of birth and death fragmented and mortared into its corners, underbellies, and seams.

In years of exceptional wind and tide, the sands at Ocean Beach shift with all of their old wildness, baring pieces of the wall at the top edge of the beach. Every few decades, beautiful granite gravestones and bits of tomb marker from the nineteenth century are found exposed along the strand, bearing the ghostly names of people who once lived here when the city was young, when the sand dunes still danced under the howling hands of wind, mysterious and unknowable people who are long since gone. Sometimes the letters are faded, sometimes they are clear. "Delia Presby, Wife of E.B. Oliver, died April 9. 1890, aged 26 yrs. 10 mos. 27 days. REST," read one gravestone, stark in the wet sand in the summer of 2012. After a few months, it was pushed and covered again by strong tides and heaving sand, lost once more to time—like the great sweeping dunescape, like the tiny powdered wings of the Xerces blue, alighting on a fragrant bush lupine for the last time.

Some gardeners claim that without irrigation or fertilizer, Golden Gate Park would return to dunes in a matter of ten years. Always underneath the city there are the ghosts of sand dunes; there are chrysalises that never hatched; there are seeds that will wait forever if they must, hoping to bloom again.

Yellow lupines growing on the sand dunes of early San Francisco. Courtesy of the San Francisco History Center, San Francisco Public Library

Opposite page: The growing Richmond District seen from Lone Mountain in 1908. Courtesy of the California Historical Society

Miners gathered near the Central Mine in Stewartville in 1888. Courtesy of the Black Diamond Mines Regional Preserve, Edna Gibble Collection

Mount Diablo Coal Mines

It is hard to imagine what the miners felt when they came up out of the heart of Mount Diablo at dusk. It is hard to imagine the kind of darkness they held their small candles and oil lamps to all day, or the weight of so much mountain above their heads. Humans are not meant to spend a day—let alone days, year after year—deep underground. Emerging into the soft breeze above ground at the end of each shift must have been a very sweet and simple kind of miracle.

Coal was discovered beneath the northern flanks of Mount Diablo in 1859 when a local rancher struck a vein while cleaning out one of his springs, and disgruntled argonauts weary of gold panning flocked to the site, ready to make a steadier profit by this dark treasure. Family after family followed, not only old gold rush diggers, but immigrants seeking work from all over the world—Wales and Italy, Germany, China, Scotland and Australia, Mexico, Canada, Austria. They planted trees from their home countries—black locust, cypress, tree of heaven, pepper tree—like prayers: that they too might grow roots and branches and flourish here where it was dry, here where at night the sky was huge and speckled and strange and the coyotes howled.

Five towns were sparked into existence by the mountain's coal, growing up quick as flame around the three seams on Mount Diablo's foothills. The towns were Nortonville, Somersville, Judsonville, Stewartville, and West Hartley, all stark against the steep, dusty hills. They clustered in separate valleys around the coalfields, though each was within easy walking distance of the next on footpaths and narrow roads that led up and over the dry hills. Nortonville was the largest (with nine hundred residents by 1870) and the most centrally located of the five, with Somersville next beyond the eastern ridge. Stewartsville lay further east beyond Somersville, and the smallest two settlements, Judsonville and West Hartley, were built all the way at the furthest eastern edge of the mines. It must have seemed, to the chamise and sagebrush and manzanita that grew on the ridges, as though the five mining towns were slapped up overnight. One day dry hills, the next day clapboard butcher's shop, boardinghouse, post office, a dozen little Victorian cottages with

Black Diamond Mine outside Nortonville circa 1880.

Opposite page, top: Nortonville boardinghouses and homes.

Opposite page, bottom: Looking down Main Street in Nortonville in the 1870s.

All photographs courtesy of the California Historical Society

Nortonville, looking west in the 1870s. Courtesy of the Black Diamond Mines Regional Preserve, George Vivian Collection

sapling trees from around the world, growing fast. By a count taken on February 26, 1870, 315 men worked the veins in the Mount Diablo coalfields, from coal cutters and miners to engineers, underground foremen to minecart drivers and furnace men. There were twelve mines total, accessed by steep shafts and tunnels, and centered around three primary veins: Clark, Little, and Black Diamond.

Despite the darkness that the miners endured day after day digging coal inside the mountain, there was a lively brightness to the towns that belied the grim reality underground. Walking home down the mountain, swinging their round lunch pails and stretching in the gentle evening, the men might have caught a whiff of baking bread—fourteen loaves twice a week!—made by Amelia Ginichio at her family's boardinghouse on Italian Hill. Or they might have glimpsed the white horse named Jim making his rounds throughout Nortonville with grocer and cart to drop off food and supplies requested in the morning. Maybe, going their separate ways on paths through the foothills, some of them were passed by a speeding horse and cart—

midwife Sarah Norton inside—rushing off to attend a birth. In the course of her life, the wife of Nortonville's founder was said to have delivered six hundred babies without losing a single one.

Down in the towns there were barbershops in which to clean up, billiard saloons in which to unwind, and for those miners who wished to further their education, there were evening classes offered by local schools. Many men religiously attended these classes, even after a ten-hour day underground, especially those who had left school for the mines when they were only boys to help support their families. Fraternal organizations abounded, from the Sons of Temperance, the Masonic lodge, and the Grand Army of the Republic, to the Ancient Order of United Workmen. According to visitors, the Mount Diablo coal towns were positively lively; Somersville boasted two excellent hotels with room for up to one hundred boarders, several stores, and a billiard saloon, not to mention a very good public school system. And for all the men working underground, there were nearly as many wives, daughters, or mothers working above ground. Women ran suffrage societies and worked as postmistresses, schoolteachers, and hotel proprietors, not to mention the daily work of tending house, garden, and livestock.

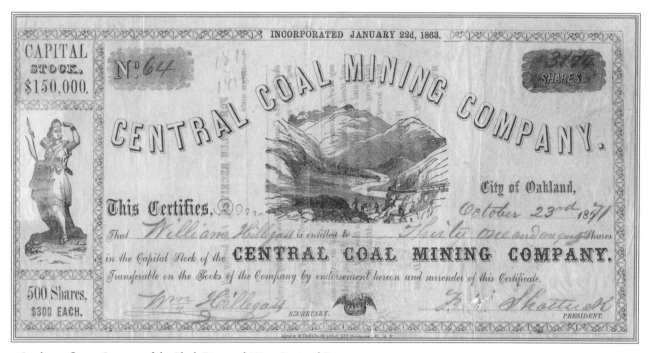

Stock certificate. Courtesy of the Black Diamond Mines Regional Preserve

Rose Hill Cemetery in the hills between Somersville and Nortonville. Courtesy of the Black Diamond Mines Regional Preserve

For those with loved ones in the mines, no doubt this daily work was often accompanied by a small prayer—that another dusk would arrive without incident underground. There were periodic tunnel cave-ins, as earth and stone collapsed without warning in great sighs of mountain weight. Sometimes, loose coal dust was ignited by a spark or candle flame, causing devastating explosions, or carts loaded with coal snapped their ropes, crushing whoever happened to be behind them. The insides of mines are laced with sudden seeps of deadly gas (called damps by miners: firedamp, blackdamp, whitedamp, stinkdamp, afterdamp), which cause asphyxiation, explosions, or both. Miners were equipped with flame safety lamps, which served as both light and warning signal, but according to a report in an 1874 edition of the *Contra Costa Gazette,* the light was feeble compared to other lamps that the men used, and many were willing to risk their

Seven unidentified children pose in front of the fence that surrounds the Black Diamond Coal Company stables outside Nortonville, looking south circa 1880. Courtesy of the Black Diamond Mines Regional Preserve, George Vivian Collection

lives rather than bother with the inconvenience and unease of poor light far down inside the earth. Many preferred the simplicity of a candlestick inside a can (called a bug light), or an oil wick lamp affixed to the front of a cap. The Rose Hill Cemetery attests to the danger of work in the mines, as most of the burials are either of young men—such as the eleven lost in an 1876 explosion caused when loose coal dust was ignited by a seep of methane four hundred feet deep

in the mines. Otherwise, most of the graves belong to babies lost to childhood illnesses.

Still, work was work, and Mount Diablo's young, subbituminous coal was abundant, occurring in great, dark layers, so that from the 1860s to the early 1900s, four million tons were hauled up to the light and burned in Northern California. Mount Diablo coal lit the woodstove of virtually every home throughout the Bay Area, warming the feet of mining investors and

dairy lords, prostitutes and laborers and bakers alike. Every factory, steamship, ferry, and mill around ran on the stuff too. By the 1870s, trains came and went daily, crossing five miles each way on tracks as straight as an engineer's ruler, from the foothills of Mount Diablo to the banks of the San Joaquin River delta.

Less than fifty years after the first coal was dug, the towns and coal mines were virtually empty. A flash of digging, dancing, praying, loving, and striving over barely two generations—and then nothing. Families followed the coal, and a new mountain far up north in Washington provided a finer, bituminous variety. The Columbia Steel Corporation discovered silica near Nortonville in the 1920s, and started mining the deep,

thick sandstone beds for foundry sand. Soon enough, glass-worthy silica was uncovered near Somersville, and by the 1930s, the Hazel-Atlas Glass Company was shipping the raw minerals for glassware to their Oakland bottle-making factory. Still, the towns were never fully occupied again, and far below, deep down in the heart of the mountain, the coal remains, untroubled by human hands.

We are playing with fire when we dig out the hearts of mountains. We are playing with fate, with faulty lanterns held aloft. But people being people, there will always be dancing between, and dozens of loaves of fresh bread.

Miners in Somersville circa 1870, holding candlesticks and bug lights (candles inside cans). Courtesy of the Black Diamond Mines Regional Preserve, Kay Serrano Collection

Opposite page: The Pittsburg Railroad, loaded up with coal, leaving Somersville. Courtesy of the Black Diamond Mines Regional Preserve, Oakland Museum Collection

Gulls flocking over a rocky hill on the Southeast Farallon Island in 1954. Courtesy of the San Francisco History Center, San Francisco Public Library

The Farallon Lighthouse

If you see your name scribbled on the shell of a common murre egg, you've been on the island too long. That's what lighthouse keepers and their families liked to say to visitors who came to Southeast Farallon Island, perhaps over a breakfast of said eggs. Their texture—and red yolks—took a little getting used to, but if the island was truly home to anyone, it was home to seabirds, and the lighthouse keepers had little else to reap from the talus crags besides the eggs of countless murres. The morning view from the lighthouse's front windows looked out over a flat, granitic marine terrace and straight to the snarling Pacific, blue as lapis and thick with great white sharks. Behind the two main houses, where four families lived at a time (two per house), the island sloped steeply up to a 348-foot peak and the lighthouse, perched above it all. There was truly no protection here from the sudden gales that whipped off the ocean, so strong that the paint was perpetually peeling off the houses, and fine bits of granite got lodged into the wood. Nor was there protection from the racing spring winds, nor the endless granite itself, which was so rough to walk over that shoes had to be replaced, entirely shredded, after two months.

It was more like inhabiting a very large rock than an island. The Farallones, thirty miles west of the Golden Gate, are little more than a jagged range of granite teeth sticking up out of the wild ocean, at the edge of the continental shelf just before the ocean floor drops six thousand feet. It is truly the edge of the world. Lighthouse keepers only ever inhabited Southeast Farallon Island, the biggest of the bunch at a whopping 0.12 square miles; the others are just sharp rocks, impossible to navigate, much less land upon, unless you are a seal or a bird. Even Southeast Farallon, plenty big enough for a dock, could never sustain one because the water around its perimeter was too rough, and most boats that attempted it were smashed against the marine terrace. The only way to get onto the island was to leap from a small boat to the slippery rocks with a prayer in your teeth, or else to be hitched, small craft and all, to a derrick that swung you out high over the ocean before hoisting you up to rocky land. The latter option was hardly safer, as the whole contraption more than once snapped and broke into the ocean in wild weather.

A bird's-eye view of the Southeast Farallon Island in 1960. Courtesy of the San Francisco History Center, San Francisco Public Library

Passengers being hoisted from a sling and boom onto the Southeast Farallon Island in 1939.

Inset: A close-up of the sling and boom operation and its passengers.

Both photographs courtesy of the San Francisco History Center, San Francisco Public Library

And yet, there was a lighthouse that needed tending. So people, living where only seabirds and seals have ever thrived, managed to survive and raise families for more than one hundred years—from 1855 until 1969. On April 8, 1898, the first human child was born on this small perch out in the thrashing sea, one Farallone Cain. Of course, for centuries the Farallones had been a breeding ground for non-human babies, and on their crags and cliffs and shores millions of seabirds and pinnipeds found respite enough from the ocean tides to birth and tend their children. Here, on ledges jutting sheer over the rocking troughs of the lapis Pacific, common murres nested side by side on the cliffs and flats by the hundreds of thousands, laying conical eggs so wonderfully suited to the terrain that they could balance in their stony nests without rolling or falling. Puffins, auklets, cormorants, storm petrels, gulls, and guillemots nested here too. Mammals found safety here as well; elephant seals, sea lions, harbor seals, and even fur seals hauled up onto the marine terrace for millennia to birth and nurse their pups.

And so, to seabird and pinniped alike, these islands were not desolate wastelands of wind and granite and relentless boredom, as lighthouse keepers must often have thought, but rather a kind of paradise, rich in food and shelter both. For not only are the Farallones located right along the much travelled migration route between Baja and Alaska, they are also situated in the Gulf of the Farallones, where spring winds and cold upwelling from the ocean bottom charge the waters with plankton of all varieties, turning them into the craggy seats of a banquet hall. Of course, with the arrival first of Russian fur traders in the early 1800s

Lighthouse at Farallon circa 1875 by Carleton E. Watkins. Courtesy of the Pat Hathaway Collection

Opposite page. Top left: Murres nesting on the steep, granite outcrops of the Farallones.

Top right: Sea lions along the west end of the Southeast Farallon.

Bottom left: Two men smoking long pipes on the Low Arch, Southeast Farallon Island.

Bottom right: Lighthouse on the Southeast Farallon Island.

All photographs by Carleton E. Watkin circa 1861–1873. Courtesy of the California Historical Society

Egg pickers at work on the Farallones filling their baskets with murre and gull eggs circa 1880.
Courtesy of the San Francisco Maritime National Historical Park

and later egg hunters from gold rush San Francisco, people wanted in on the natural bounty too.

The results were nothing short of catastrophic for bird and seal alike. By the time lighthouse keepers arrived on Southeast Farallon in 1855, sea otters and elephant seals were all but gone from its waters, and from all of California, hunted into virtual extinction for their furs and fats. The common murre population, devastated by the theft of millions of eggs to feed San Francisco's booming, if food-poor population, took a steady nosedive until all of the islands were at last declared a marine sanctuary in 1969.

Before the lighthouse, the Farallones posed a serious danger to all ships headed for the Golden Gate, as the waters around the islands were notoriously dangerous and the rocks themselves nearly impossible to see at night until it was far too late. Once the gold rush turned San Francisco into a bustling port, with ships coming and going daily, the hazard posed by the islands became too dangerous to ignore. By 1852, lighthouses all around the Golden Gate had been commissioned and were underway. But building on the Farallones was easier said than done. As Major Hartman Bache wrote to the Lighthouse Board after surveying the peak upon which he'd been commissioned to build the Farallon lighthouse in 1854, "the operation is second only to impossible" due to the steep pitch of the hill leading to the future lighthouse site, the treacherous, sharp

The Southeast Farallon Island, with the lighthouse at its peak in 1943. Courtesy of the San Francisco History Center, San Francisco Public Library

Supplies being pushed along the railroad track that ran from marine terrace to lighthouse cottages in 1926.
Courtesy of the San Francisco History Center, San Francisco Public Library

footing, and the fact that men had to carry bricks up on their backs in loads of only four or five.

Much to the chagrin of its workers, the Farallon lighthouse had to be built twice. The first structure, completed in 1853, had to be torn down when the long-awaited Fresnel lens arrived from France—in seventy-three crates—and was found to be too big to fit the tower. The lens was a beautiful piece of crafts-manship, designed in sheets of thin glass arranged in concentric, prismatic layers that caught and reflected light with great intensity. A second tower was built, this time made to fit the lens. But even once that great glass light was flashing regularly out over the wild sea, ship-wrecks still plagued the waters around the Farallones when the fog was dense. A foghorn was needed, but this wouldn't arrive until 1880, due to the logistics of running a coal-operated steam plant in such a remote location.

Until then, the only warning sailors had of the near-ness of the Farallones on a foggy day was the maniac sound of a train whistle, which the ever-resourceful Bache had rigged to a sea cave with a blow hole in the top. When waves pounded and pushed air out of the hole, their force would blow the whistle. Of course, when there was only fog but no wind, the whistle was dead silent, and when wind accompanied a clear day, as it most often did, the whistle blew and blew, likely driving the lighthouse keepers half mad with its shrill sound. Between the train whistle, the absolute granitic barrenness of the island, and the incessant clamoring of gulls, one can only imagine what life was like. Light-house keepers with families were favored over single men because the Lighthouse Board was aware that the utter isolation and barrenness of the island could easily drive lone men to madness.

So the families who lived on Southeast Farallon contrived to create some semblance of normalcy out of their island life. Rainwater was collected in barrels, and a growing population of introduced rabbits provided an easy source of meat and fur. The downside to the rabbits was that they ate the only green thing growing on the island, a little flowering herb called seaside gold-fields, or Farallon weed, which thrived on bird guano. But they were also a favorite item to barter with the fishermen who sometimes passed through, delighted by the taste of rabbit after days of fish. Women kept small gardens outside the two main houses, with soil shipped in from the mainland, and goats, pigs, and chickens roamed the grounds freely, as there was little reason to worry about them escaping. Mules helped with the heavy labor up and down the rocky peaks. Islanders treasured what small comforts they could find, including a spring only a few feet above the surf that seeped water tasting like sour lemonade, which was prized for its supposedly curative properties. A drink from Amber Spring (named for the color of its water) was said to be a cure-all for stomach ailments. But then there were the red-yolk eggs for breakfast, and the endless sharp guano-streaked peaks, and the clam-oring gulls who, after a time, sounded like they were saying your name, and above it all, the lighthouse was always bright, burning whale oil and flashing safety.

The first little girl to move to the island was the four-year-old daughter of the principal keeper, who brought his family to live with him there in 1860. She was fond of calling herself "the girl of the Farallones" to any and all fishermen and tugboat captains who happened to stop by. Children loved to ride the resident mules of the Farallones, who were each, one after the next, dogged workers until their deaths, and much beloved. First Jack, then Jerry, then Patty (named for opera singer Adelina Patti), who died in 1913.

For two short years the Farallon children even had a schoolmistress, Miss Daisy Doud, who, upon her arrival, was hoisted up out of her boat by the derrick with a globe of the world in one hand and a caged flock of pigeons in the other. The pigeons would carry her letters home to the mainland. She was quick to declare boat days "national holidays," for surely she would have faced an all-out mutiny otherwise. On "boat day," the Lighthouse Service tender docked at the edge of the island, with food, coal, oil, letters, and news. It was the day island residents got a whiff of home, a taste of life out of the ceaseless and all-consuming ocean elements. Until the turn of the century, the tender only came once every three months—a wait that must sometimes have felt interminable. By the early 1900s, the boat came every two weeks. The only one who didn't love the arrival of the tender was the resident mule. Jerry was known to run and hide deep in the granite rocks when he heard the tender's whistle, because he knew it meant a long day working the windlass, which hoisted goods up and down from the precarious landing site, and then lugging them all around the island until nightfall.

The rest of the time, Farallon residents were essentially stranded on a seventy-acre smattering of granite in the middle of the wild blue churning ocean, with nowhere to hide from the bounding and violent winter storms, nor the sun, nor each other, and no one to

A little girl plays alone on the steps of her house on Southeast Farallon Island with her doll and a pet wild rabbit. *San Francisco News* photo by Eddie Murphy, 1954.

Opposite page: Fisherman's Cove on the Southeast Farallon in 1926.

Both photos courtesy of the San Francisco History Center, San Francisco Public Library

turn to in times of true emergency. And emergency did strike, most often in the form of childhood illnesses such as diphtheria, scarlet fever, and typhoid. In such cases, families hoisted distress flags and then had to pray for the passing of a random fisherman, tugboat, or coast guard ship. As often as not, these flags were ignored, and many children died there on the lonesome, rocky island where the wind had the last song and the ocean thrashed without pause.

By the middle of the twentieth century, Southeast Farallon hosted not only a lighthouse but also a navy weather station, four radio facilities, and, by World War II, a secret radar station. After the war, the waters off the rocks of the Farallones became the dumping site for the Atomic Energy Commission's radioactive waste,

mostly lab materials, which amounted to nearly fifty thousand containers. Between this, and the century-long assault on the island's bird and mammal life by human occupation, Southeast Farallon was declared a National Wildlife Refuge in 1969, and all human visits prohibited save by marine biologists from the Point Reyes Bird Observatory. In the same year, the lighthouse was fully automated.

On a very clear day, if you peer out from some ridge in the headlands, or crossing the Golden Gate Bridge, the Farallones are a stark violet silhouette against the horizon, adrift a world apart, belonging more to humpbacks than to humans. And at long last, the seabirds and seals are kings and queens of the place once more.

Riverboats docked in Stockton. Courtesy of the San Francisco Maritime National Historical Park

Paddlewheel Boats

It is the middle of the night at the beginning of the last century, and the smell of the river rises up to the top deck, a cool scent of tules and silt. There are stars everywhere, their own river, wheeling down so close and bright they seem to rest somewhere just beyond the prow of the boat, dissolving into marsh. The music and sparkling lights, the dancing and feasting, are done; the band and the chefs and the passengers are asleep below, in cabins lined with oak. Only insomniacs and romantics are pacing the deck now. The river pilot has no time to savor scents and stars. He steers the steamboat through the dark, navigating by memory and by landmarks glimpsed dimly through the murk of water and the tule fog that rises up and drifts low against the river skin and the land—a cottonwood snag on the right with one burl like a fish; the abandoned adobe house whose empty windows are round like the eyes of owl. The paddle-wheel splashes. The smokestack hisses. The steam engine makes its gentle low calls. But the river absorbs these sounds so that they become dreamlike, and all around, on the banks, there is a susurrus of leaves. The overhanging trees grow in a thick band along the river, a tangle of cottonwoods and alders, ash and

The head of the Stockton channel, on an arm of the San Joaquin River, circa 1925. Courtesy of the California Historical Society

valley oak and willow, covered in veils of grapevines and wild currants that by daylight is a lush maze of green that simmers with the buzzing calls of willow flycatchers and the sweet, swooping songs of phoebes. White forms hunched in the trees emerge like ghosts out of the darkness. A rookery, full of a thousand roosting white egrets, great blue herons, night herons, and cormorants. The trees are heavy with their nests and their noisy cries.

In some places, the dense thicket of trees gives way to labyrinths of tules. They clack and sway, creating their own marshy islands, their own snaking corridors full of sleeping ducks. Any amount of moon that might be rising over the far mountains will turn them silver blue, with thin, long shadows. Suddenly, the boat is surrounded by throaty, grating chatter, whistles and clacks, and the heavy flapping of wings. The stars tilt.

The Sacramento waterfront, by J. B. M. Crooks & Co. Courtesy of the California Historical Society

Orion is setting now, a sideways bridge piercing the horizon. The Pleiades sparkle. The decks are empty now of even the worst insomniacs, and all is still save the gentle hush and splash of the boat through the dark green night.

By dawn, as passengers yawn and stretch to the morning light coming through their cabin windows, and make their way upstairs for a hearty breakfast, the boat will already have been docked in Sacramento for several hours, all of its city cargo unloaded, ready for the return journey full of fruit and grain.

Beyond the river and the steady pace of the paddle-wheel boat, the Sacramento Valley stretched out in every direction, millions of acres of marsh and riparian woodland so full of plant and animal life that it defied the senses. A Serengeti, it was once called, with a beauty that—as the San Joaquin Valley Agricultural Society wrote in 1861—"carried the weary eye away into the hazy limits of the tule world, where the mingled tints of green and blue formed rainbow galaxies of Earth's creation." Soon after the gold rush, the dense, lush, watery forests along the Sacramento River became home to many diverse human communities. Hermits lived among the cottonwoods, seeking peaceful lives away from the rush for gold and the growing cacophony of the city. Chinese fisherman caught salmon and

The *Julia,* a paddlewheel boat docked in Stockton in 1870. Courtesy of the San Francisco Maritime National Historical Park

Opposite page, top: The main cabin of the *City of Sacramento,* looking aft. Courtesy of the San Francisco Maritime National Historical Park, Skibinsky Collection

Opposite page, bottom: The passenger area of the *City of Sacramento,* built in 1903. Courtesy of the San Francisco Maritime National Historical Park, Skibinksy Collection

trout, and sold them to the miners preserved in salt. Day laborers stripped bark off the oaks to send back to San Francisco to be used in tanneries. Newly built dikes, dams, and levees opened more and more land for agriculture, from grains to fruit trees. Golden beavers and mink did their best to hide among the rushes from fur hunters, but their pelts fetched a high price, and ducks and geese of a dozen species were hunted in short cedar boats known as tule splitters that darted among the marshes, bagging goldeneyes and northern shoveler ducks, white-fronted geese and coots, to be sold to restaurants in San Francisco. White egrets were hunted for their long feathers, which were used in ladies' hats.

The steam-run paddlewheel boat was a gold rush innovation. There was no formal road from San Francisco to the diggings in the Sierra foothills, and those who did try to travel across the Central Valley's labyrinthine marshes often found themselves lost in a gleaming green tule maze, boots soaking, hooves sunk in mud. The Sacramento River and its waterways provided a direct and relatively easy route from the San Francisco Bay to the foothills, where a stagecoach or an oxcart might be hired for the final leg of the journey. The boats were never solely for the men racing to the mountains with gold pans. They also hauled freight upriver—building materials, mining equipment, farm implements—and carried agricultural goods such as canned fruit, great sacks of rice and wheat, and crates of gold back to the city.

"Prospectors, Chinamen, empire-builders, gunmen, tinhorns, and trollops; rural blades bound for the delights of the City, Kanakas, bindle stiffs, merchants, bankers, and Filipino farm-hands; turbaned Hindus on their way to the rice fields—their passenger lists were nothing if not cosmopolitan," writes Jerry MacMullen in his 1944 *Paddle-Wheel Days in California*. There was an open friendliness to the whole affair, a coming together of many people and many worlds on those wide decks. One riverboat pilot named Johnny Myrick—who must have been an extraordinary fellow indeed—allowed a handful of Sacramento housewives to give him shopping lists and the requisite sums of money, so that he might comb the shops of San Francisco for them, and bring back the articles they desired. He didn't charge a dime for the effort or his time, and was remembered well into the 1940s, his name famous among the green waters and the quiet delta wharves.

For a time, travel by paddlewheel boat was rather expensive. Like everything in San Francisco, the price of the ticket was inflated by sacks of gold dust. It was also, in those early days, not entirely safe. Boilers had a habit of exploding—on the *Sagamore* in 1851, the *Washoe* in 1864, and the *Yosemite* in 1865—killing dozens of people each time. When the steamboats began to use oil instead of wood, deadly fires often broke out on board, fueled by so many barrels of waiting petroleum. But neither the danger nor the price seemed to stop passengers from crowding on board, and soon both boilers and costs improved, so that by the 1920s, you could rent the big stateroom for five dollars, the smallest cabin for one dollar. During the Great Depression, you could travel from San Francisco to Sacramento and back again for only $1.95.

Top left: The *Julia,* seen underway in the Mare Island Strait near Vallejo circa 1895. Courtesy of the San Francisco Maritime National Historical Park. Top right: The *Ocean Wave,* built in 1891. Courtesy of the San Francisco History Center, San Francisco Public Library. Bottom left: The *Tamalpais* circa 1941. Courtesy of the San Francisco History Center, San Francisco Public Library. Bottom right: A painting of the *El Capitan* ferryboat, one of San Francisco and Oakland's steamers from the 1870s and '80s. Courtesy of the San Francisco History Center, San Francisco Public Library

In 1927, paddlewheel boats reached the pinnacle of elegance and luxury in the *Delta King* and the *Delta Queen,* twin boats (one for each harbor up and down river) that sailed every day without fail for thirteen years, crossing paths on quiet water in the dead of night near Rio Vista. Although cargo was always more financially viable than passengers, these steamers were decked out with lavish sitting rooms paneled in old English oak, social halls lit with brass chandeliers, stained glass above port and starboard windows for viewing the river, fresh flowers on all the dining room tables, and a grand staircase with a mahogany handrail that climbed to the upper deck. They were crafted to please their passengers, to offer a river journey that dazzled the eyes and soothed the mind. Included was a feast fit for a king, complete with fresh fish and game

A steamer docked along the Sacramento waterfront circa 1880. Courtesy of the California Historical Society

The San Francisco Ferry Building on East Street in 1896. Courtesy of the San Francisco Maritime National Historical Park

birds, enormous oysters, local vegetables and champagne. After dinner, chairs and tables were shoved aside for hours of dancing. For breakfast, one could expect a stout cup of coffee and a steaming array of pastries.

To wake up docked at the edge of sleepy Sacramento, with new sun flooding through the windows and the Sierra rising, snow-tipped, to the east, and red-winged blackbirds rattling in the marsh; to have a strong coffee up on the deck where the river below stretched broad and calm and green, so different than the gray wavelets on the cold and salty San Francisco Bay the evening before—it was a slower, quieter world, when the rivers were our roads.

It was the advent of trucks as cargo carriers, and the freeways they were made for, that spelled the demise of the paddlewheel boat. For many years, old steamers sat hitched like forgotten horses at the docks in Stockton and Sacramento. Some became restaurants, others clubhouses. Fires along the waterfront claimed several, and the breakneck pace of highway trucking claimed the rest, all save a handful that remain as museum pieces, dreaming still of the river and of star-thick nights with only the steam engine for a song.

A view of China Camp from north of Point San Pedro on the San Pablo Bay, taken in 1888. Courtesy of the California Historical Society

Shrimp Fishing at China Camp

The smell of salt is constant, the sound of the soft and rocking tide ceaseless. A brown pelican flies low over the water, past the deep marshes where pickleweed and saltgrass grow, their shadows on the water iridescent, wavering. The long arms of the San Pablo Ridge, densely packed with black oak, bay laurel, and madrone, slope down toward the bay and shelter the coves from summer fogs. Meanwhile, at the hem of the land, the mud and the marsh grasses betray little movement, and the great white egrets hunt with a slow and graceful patience. But the marshes quietly teem. Below, the mud is full of countless different species of clams, tunneling worms, and tiny crabs, and the shallow waters are nurseries for six species of grass shrimp, all key players in the bay's food chain. They form a blue seam of nourishment beneath the moving tide and the many-colored marsh.

It must always have felt something like this, even in the 1880s, when the shores bustled with the more than two dozen of the Chinese shrimp camps that thrived around the bay.

Everyone eats shrimp, from diving cormorants to sea bass, from Dungeness crabs to red snappers. It's no wonder that so many of the indigenous people of the Bay Area spent a good portion of each year in villages along the bayshore, feasting on clams, fish, and shrimp, scooped up easily in a basket out of the tidal marsh (though their shells are too delicate to have survived in shellmounds for archeologists to find as hard proof). Grass shrimp were once so abundant that any old net dipped into the water during the right season came up heavy with their little speckled bodies. It is said that this is how the first of the bay's twenty-six Chinese shrimp camps began: some homesick and hungry fisherman in post–gold rush San Francisco dipped a net in the bay just to see what might happen. Lo, it came up dripping with shrimp.

By the 1860s, with little work left panning gold, Chinese laborers flocked to the new shrimp camps that were fast popping up around the perimeter of the bay, from Hunters Point to Richmond and all the way north to the mouth of the Petaluma River. They were mostly from the Guangdong Province on the South China Sea coast, where fishing was central to life and shrimp a mainstay of the diet. The camps they erected along the marsh edge were insular, like small villages from the old country transposed onto the tule and mudflats of the San Francisco Bay. Only Cantonese was spoken, Chinese vegetables were grown in neat garden plots, and all nets and boats were built in the traditional Chinese way. These camps were overseen by Chinese shrimp companies, all of which sent the bulk of their catch back to China, neatly dried and packaged. Most other camps housed men only, generally no more than

fifty or a hundred at a time. China Camp was the largest of these communities, home to five hundred men, women, and children by 1880. It boasted a barbershop, a general store, gardens, and even a schoolroom. Redwood cottages nestled near the shore, simple but comfortable. Words of encouragement or blessing were painted in bold calligraphy and tacked up on the walls of workrooms where the fishermen processed their daily haul. *Safety on land and sea. Get what you wish. Peace and Prosperity.*

Life was measured in tides, and in the life cycles of shrimp. Mainly younger shrimp were harvested in the shallows of the bay. They made their way to the

A China Camp alleyway. Undated.
Courtesy of the San Francisco Maritime National Historical Park

Opposite page: A China Camp fishing boat circa 1900. Courtesy of the Pat Hathaway Collection

A bayside shack at China Camp, photographed by Challiss Gore. Courtesy of the California Historical Society

sheltered marsh edges from their birthplaces out in the open ocean, getting there however they could—on tides, crawling through the mud, swimming furiously. There they took refuge in the gentle brackish water and found easy nourishment near the shore until they were strong enough to brave the salt and colder water once more, this time to spawn. The females left the protected coves when the winter rains began, swimming straight out to the middle of the bay or beyond the mouth of the Golden Gate to the Gulf of the Farallones, where eager males were waiting out in the saltier, pure ocean water. Once their tiny pearlescent eggs were laid far out in the open water—two thousand to eight thousand at a time—the cycle began again: tiny shrimp hatching and shedding several skins before heading back to the brackish shallows.

And so it was primarily the young shrimp that were flushed into bag nets tacked down in the mud, staked so they were open to the oncoming tide. As the current slackened, men in traditional junks worked over the low sides of their ships to raise the nets (which weighed between seventy and ninety pounds) and dump the fresh shrimp into baskets in the hold. Large shrimp were immediately sorted from small, and fish accidentally pulled up in the net were either kept for food or thrown back into the bay. Then the nets were set in the opposite direction to catch the shrimp pulled out with the next tidal cycle. Sixty nets might be laid out in one area, after which there was plenty of time to rest and wait.

Junks, each with a crew of four to six men, would circle close together as the tide changed and someone would set to making tea and cooking a hearty meal.

The lull between tides, between the currents of work, meant time to chat and hold a warm cup in your hands as the water rocked at the hull, the pelicans flew low, cormorants hunted, and the surface of the bay changed color with the day. The junks must have been a sight to behold, huddled together between tides like a flock of exquisite waterfowl, nearly identical to the ships of Guangdong. At forty to fifty feet in length, they had low, broad, short-hulled redwood bodies that could be worked in water as shallow as four feet, with high, flat decks built to allow workers to safely lean over the edges. They were equipped with oars for calm weather, but normally used a five-batten lugsail, a broad and tapered wing of a sail dyed dark red-brown with tan-oak bark to protect the cloth. The rudder was carved with diamond-shaped holes, both for ease of navigation and because the diamond was a symbol of good

The *City of Papeete* schooner, built in 1883, laid up off China Camp in 1944. Courtesy of the San Francisco Maritime National Historical Park, Warren Roll Collection

luck. The result was something utterly apart from the other ships that fished the bay during the 1800s. These were vessels that bore all of the elegance of another world and another culture; they proudly carried their own story out into the bay with the nets.

After two full tides—a span of roughly twelve hours—the junks returned to shore to process their haul. Sometimes it was the middle of the night when they came back to the camp, but crews worked in shifts and were ready at all hours to handle the latest load. The larger shrimp were immediately unloaded from baskets onto a waiting junk to be sent live to San Francisco's Chinatown. These were still small shrimp by modern standards, nothing like the fat prawns one finds in a shrimp cocktail; the grass shrimp of the bay are little and succulent and wild.

The rest were poured into boilers and cooked with a good scoop of coarse salt for about fifteen minutes. Cloths were laid both inside and outside, all over the bare hills, and shrimp were spread there to dry, hauled up from the boilers in great basket loads. During the height of shrimping, the hillsides at China Camp were almost constantly covered in a glinting patchwork of shrimp-cloths, and the air smelled like the salt drying off their shells. After a few days, a wooden cleat was rolled over the dry shrimp to separate the heads and shells from the meat, at which point they were hoisted back down the hills to the center of the village, where they were put through a traditional winnowing machine known as a fanning mill—a two-thousand-year-old Chinese design invented for winnowing grain—that separated the meat from the shells. A hand crank turned wooden blades that created an air cur-

A traditional shrimp mill at China Camp with Chinese characters painted on the side circa 1888 or 1889. Courtesy of the San Francisco Maritime National Historical Park

rent; crushed shrimp fell down into the current, and while light shells and heads blew away, the meat fell down to the bottom to be collected in baskets, where it was quickly bagged and loaded onto ships bound for the Chinese market.

The Chinese shrimp fishers, standing outside the rush and hum of industrial-era San Francisco—or perhaps because of this distance, this loyalty to tradition and language and home—suffered intense discrimination almost from the beginning. Even in 1862, when the shrimp camps had only just been established, white fishermen tried but failed to get restrictions passed on Chinese shrimpers. In 1880, attempts were made to completely outlaw Chinese shrimp fishing in California, but the real blow came in 1882 when the Chinese Exclusion Act was signed into law, banning all immigration of Chinese laborers to the United States.

A Chinese shrimper laying out nets along McNear's Beach. Undated.
Courtesy of the San Francisco Maritime National Historical Park, J. E. Dewey Collection

Then, in 1888, the US government passed the Scott Act, which meant that even legal residents would be denied reentry if they left the country. Many thousands of Chinese laborers who were outside the United States were unable to return. These laws severely crippled the shrimp fishing communities in the Bay Area. From the 1880s onward, state officials did everything they could to call into question or ban Chinese shrimping methods, which were blamed for the declining health of the bay. It is true that millions of pounds of shrimp, a species critical to all life in the bay, had been harvested from its waters since the 1860s. But during the same years the bay suffered an onslaught of intense silt runoff from hydraulic mining in the Sierra, streams of untreated sewage and industrial toxins from the growing cities of San Francisco and Oakland, and the extensive diking of its marshes for farmland, which laid waste to thousands of acres of shrimp and fish nurseries. If the shrimpers were to blame, they were far from the only culprits.

In 1900, there were only 122 people at China Camp, 79 of them fishermen. When bag nets were outlawed in 1911, the era of the Chinese shrimp camp went with them. When shrimp fishing enjoyed a brief resurgence in the 1930s with the use of motorboats and beam trawls, nobody said a word about environmental degradation now that the industry was largely out of the hands of the Chinese.

The shrimp camp at Point San Pablo, as seen through the branches of eucalyptus trees. Courtesy of the San Francisco Maritime National Historical Park, J. E. Dewey Collection

But on the shores of the old China Camp village in present-day China Camp State Park, a single living thread of that lost world remains. Ninety-year-old Frank Quan, whose grandparents and parents lived and worked here from the 1880s on, lives in one of the redwood houses that remain along the shore, a little shack that once belonged to his aunt. Quan is China Camp's last and only resident. He walks the dock daily to tend to his boat or take it out to shrimp, listening to the slow rock-lap of tide, smelling the salt and wind. There are hardly any shrimp left to be caught now, he says. Although the bay has changed, and the historic China Camp is all but gone—save a few cottages and a vegetable garden, a small museum, and an old, boarded-up café unchanged since the 1950s, when Quan's aunt and mother ran it—Frank Quan and his family have born witness to its transformations, keeping the old stories alive.

Chinese shrimpers off McNear's Beach near China Camp. Undated. Courtesy of the San Francisco Maritime National Historical Park, J. E. Dewey Collection

Two men and a dog walking through California redwoods along a lumber railway. Courtesy of the California Historical Society

The Last Days of Oakland's Redwoods

There is a quality of silence under redwood trees that cannot be named. It is not just the floor of thick, orange-needled duff and how it absorbs all footfalls into its own quiet, nor is it simply the way the light changes, softening and darkening to a cadence more candle than sun. It is not size alone either, though the great old giants in the Oakland hills originally reached more than thirty feet in diameter, thriving on slightly more inland sun and warmth than their coastal kin. To be in the presence of living things so enormous is its own conversation with the deep time of this earth, and therefore an intense encounter with all that is mysterious and vast. The quality of quiet peace that descends when you enter a redwood grove comes from the sum of all these together, the way trees create their own world of sound and light and time. Because of the way they grow—close and thick—and gather fog in their branches and drip it down to their roots, the climate in a redwood forest is cooler than all surrounding areas; they, in a sense, engineer their own weather. And because of the acidity of the soil they create with their leaf humus, and the strength of their shallow but thick roots, only a select community of other plants can grow in redwood shade.

To venture into that spiced and ancient grove is truly to step into an older rhythm of time, one made by the trees themselves.

Such silence lasted for millennia. In the hills east of Oakland, a pocket of ancient and enormous redwoods thrived just where the ocean fog reached and rested, in a small band spanning the ridge from present-day Redwood and Leona parks east to Moraga—roughly five square miles of dense, old-growth forest. Because redwoods crown sprout from stumps and the roots of fallen ancestors, the age of such a forest is almost inconceivable—while a 32-foot broad, 300-foot tall tree might represent a millennium of vertical growth, the genetics and rootstock below might span many thousands, if not millions, of years. But it took little more than fifteen years, from 1845 to 1860, for crews of loggers to level the entire forest. Even many of the stumps were dug out and cut into cords of firewood or shingles, preventing the next generation from crown sprouting around its old grandfather. Only one original tree remains today, a twisted runt of an old-growth redwood, ninety-three feet tall, growing miraculously out of a rock on a cliff face near Merritt College and probably too difficult to reach, or to catch as it fell, for loggers to bother.

Long before they were logged, the redwoods along the ridge were well known by sailors. Two giants, called the Navigation Trees, stood at the edge of a grove, silhouetted stark against the horizon, and were first recorded by British navy captain Frederick William Beechey in 1826. He discovered that in order to avoid collision with Blossom Rock, an underwater island visible only at low tide, and safely land in the

Frederick William Beechey portrait by George Duncan Beechey, painted circa 1822. Courtesy of the National Maritime Museum, Greenwich, London

San Francisco harbor he must line up the tip of Yerba Buena Island with "two trees on the top of the hills too conspicuous to be ignored." They must have been massive, to be spotted clearly from the mouth of the Golden Gate sixteen miles away. When the Navigation Trees were logged after 1855, the army blew up Blossom Rock in order to avoid shipwrecks.

Oakland's enormous redwoods were not easy trees to fell, due not only to their size but also to their location up steep and roadless canyons. A handful were cut here and there before 1850, mainly by two French

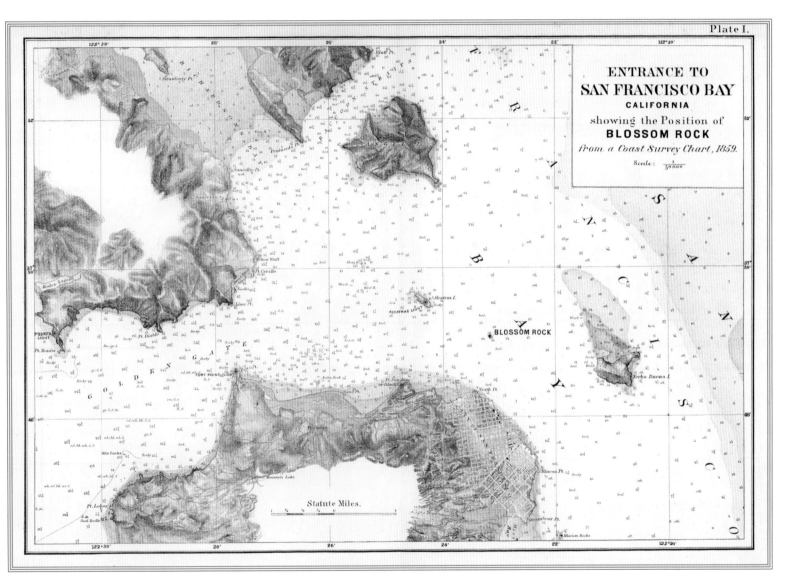

An 1859 survey chart of the entrance to the San Francisco Bay, with the dangerous Blossom Rock prominently marked for the benefit of navigators. Courtesy of the David Rumsey Map Collection

A rough-and-ready California lumbering crew. Courtesy of the California Historical Society

A logging train in Northern California, similar to what might have been used in Oakland's redwood forests.
Freese & Fetrow photograph. Courtesy of the California Historical Society

carpenters in the early 1840s who hand-milled the wood and transported it down from the hills on small boats that navigated the streams, then across the bay to the small settlement of Yerba Buena (later San Francisco). But mostly the woods were quiet, especially after 1842, when John Sutter began milling wood in the Sierra and at Fort Ross, which he'd just purchased from the Russians, dominating the lumber business in the area for several years.

But then the year 1849 tolled its heavy golden bell and, flooded by gold-hunters from all over the world, the little town of Yerba Buena swelled beyond anyone's reckoning. San Francisco—as the little town was rechristened—was "lusty and inflammable" in the words of twentieth-century chronicler Sherwood Burgess, and it had a voracious appetite for wood. Finding gold panning less lucrative on the whole than they'd thought, weary forty-niners were soon rushing up to the hills and joining makeshift logging camps, where the arrival of the first steam sawmill on Palo Seco Creek jump-started a new era of redwood lumbering in the East Bay. More and more towns pushed up out of nowhere like mushrooms, demanding wood—Martinez, Benicia, Lafayette. The lumber port at San Antonio, which was shipping many tons of redwood lumber up and down the bay each day by the early 1850s, soon became the Port of Oakland, and the city of Oakland grew quickly around it. Virtually all east-west roads through Oakland were planned in relation to the logging camps in the hills and were used by mule and ox teams to drag wood down out of the forest to the port. The old-growth redwoods became the new towns of the East Bay and much of the city of San Francisco (including its famous cable cars) all in what, to the trees themselves, must have felt like no more than a single inhalation of time.

Roads and steam mills make the whole undertaking sound orderly and staid, but in truth the logging of the East Bay redwoods had all the characteristics of the gold rush about it and was undertaken by many of the same men. These were men "with a talent for exploitation unseen in this country before." Really, it was a savage and devastating free-for-all, each mill operator and his men racing all competitors for access to virgin stands of trees. In no time there were ten sawmills, nine of them steam powered, one powered by water.

Joseph Lamson and his daughter, to whom he wrote epistolary accounts of his time at the lumber camps among Oakland's old-growth redwoods.

Opposite page: One of Joseph Lamson's colorful letters.

Both images courtesy of the Moraga History Center

According to the diaries of Joseph Lamson, owner of a lodging house and a liquor and grocery store deep in the redwoods from 1853 to 1855, the mill workers were a rowdy, rough-dealing, hard-drinking lot, often called the "redwood boys" or the "redwood rangers," like some band of terrible and legendary outlaws. They would materialize suddenly out of the thick forest to exact their own form of justice, particularly over the loss of property. In one instance, two hundred and fifty of them emerged from the woods and surrounded the Oakland home of a man they suspected of stealing three oxen from the sawmill operator Hiram Thorn (after whom Thornhill Road in Oakland is named). They threatened him with lynching, and marched up and down the surrounding streets, rifles at the ready,

387

and mischievous boys.

Thursday 21st June. A very hot day. Mercury at 106° in the house. Suspecting that the heat in the house might be greater than in other shady places in consequence of the heated roof and the confined air, I hung the thermometer on a large and thickly leaved alder tree, where the temperature proved quite as high as in the house. The heat was intense, and all animated nature seemed to suffer from it. There was a light wind, but it came in hot and debilitating blasts, only increasing the weariness and lassitude which the heat induced. My body and limbs, and particularly my feet burned with the heat. While I sat in the shade the perspiration trickled down my face. Every animal sought the shade. I went down into a thicket of willows and alders near the house, and saw several jays panting with the heat, their bills stretched wide open, and their wings drooping and hanging loosely by their sides. The cat often came and stretched herself on the floor with open mouth and protruded tongue, and the dog laid himself quietly at rest upon the ground. But the sun went down at last, and a cool and refreshing night succeeded a wearisome lifeless day.

Friday 22d. Another hot day. Thermometer at 108°. Old Joaquin Moraga died today. His body was taken to the Mission Dolores for interment.

Monday 25. Went to San Francisco on my way to Sacramento. Rode Señor Brown's mule. I did not

RED WOOD LOG 12 FEET DIAMETER, TULARE CAL.

shouting that they would "lay the town in ashes" if the man didn't fork over payment for the lost oxen by the following day. Indeed, their menace was such that it took the intervention of the mayor, Horace Carpentier, and his offer of money out of the city's own coffers, to set the matter straight. Lamson's diary descriptions of rattlesnake barbeques and the infamous Hannah—a "Kanaka Lady" who rode bareback through the redwoods in her straw hat and calico dress amusing the men—begin to sound slightly fantastical, cloaked in the extravagance of bandit legends. And yet his notes are the only remaining firsthand record of this strange and violent time, impressions scrawled at the far edges of settled society, and must be taken as such. There, cloaked in the old darkness of redwoods, the logging camps seemed to become a kind of no-man's-land, where only the toughest customers ventured.

A circa 1893 oxen team similar to those that dragged lumber out of the Oakland hills.

Opposite page, top: Loggers with a felled redwood in Northern California.

Opposite page, bottom: A redwood tree twelve feet in diameter, logged in Tulare. Trees of similar size, and larger, were dragged daily out of the forests of the East Bay.

All photographs courtesy of the California Historical Society

The remains of a giant sequoia tree cut down in 1892 in Northern California. The old redwoods of the Oakland hills rivaled even the giant sequoias of the north in girth. Photograph by C. C. Curtis. Courtesy of the California Historical Society

Opposite page: Loggers sitting inside undercut circa 1890. Photograph by A. W. Ericson. Courtesy of the Pat Hathaway Collection

By 1854, the biggest trees were gone, and by 1860, all the mills had closed down. The hills were a ragged quilt of stumps. The delicate root systems of the shy understory plants, such as redwood sorrel and trillium, were so damaged by the ravages of oxen teams and the deep furrows made by the trees they dragged behind that even today, few sorrel or wake-robin communities have returned. The trees, however, regrew fast, so that by 1906, when earthquake and then fire leveled the city of San Francisco, second-growth lumber from the Oakland hills rebuilt virtually the entire city. All the redwoods now protected within Redwood Regional and Joaquin Miller Parks are a spry young third-growth generation, tiny in comparison to their ancestors, and lonesome too. No longer do giant California condors nest by the hundreds in their boughs, nor do grizzly bears come padding down through the orange-spiced duff in the dead of night to steal oxen from the pens of loggers. And the silence of redwood forest, though still palpable if you venture up a side canyon, far from any trail, has lost something of its pulse. These young trees, only a century old at most, now stand within the confines of human time. It will take thousands of years for them to become ancient giants again, with the span of stars in their embered bark.

The Town on the Hill, New Almaden 1863, by Carleton E. Watkins. Courtesy of the Getty's Open Content Program

New Almaden Quicksilver Mine

A wooden spoon clangs against a frying pan as the long, sharp whistle from the shaft house breaks through the damp and birdsong, announcing the seven o'clock shift. The coast live oaks rustling with the passage of the panadero on his mule, bearing great baskets of bread from house to house, silver bells tinkling at the bridle. Feet trudging through dust down the trails from Spanishtown and Englishtown, heading toward the mine. The wrentits and spotted towhees calling and chattering in the chaparral, a little louder as each fresh sweep of sun turns the dew to mist and then to air.

These were the sounds of early morning at New Almaden mine, tucked in a valley between the cinnabar hills of the Coast Range south of San Jose—the immediate, gentle bustle of the mining camps readying themselves for the day; the greater stillness of the big surrounding ridges, touched slowly with light. But if, as the Victorian writer, artist, and pioneer Mary Hallock Foote once imagined, you were to nestle an elaborate ear trumpet against the side of a hill, you would hear a whole other set of sounds: the clamor of hammer and drill, black powder blasts, and minecarts laboring up tracks in the vast labyrinth of tunnels,

The Washington Shaft house.

Inset: The Malacate at New Almaden circa late 1800s. *Malacate* is Spanish for windlass or hoist.

Both photographs courtesy of Santa Clara County Parks and Recreation Department, Bulmore Family Collection

The New Almaden Mine circa 1880. Courtesy of the California Historical Society

all just below the surface of that otherwise peaceful morning. "The mountain will some day be nothing but a hollow crust—a huge nut-shell, emptied of its kernel," Foote wrote in her *A California Mining Camp* in 1878; she lived for a year with her engineer husband at New Almaden, spending much of her time drawing the inhabitants, hills, and mine structures themselves.

By that time, New Almaden had already been in operation for over thirty years, and so its tunnels were indeed elaborate and far-reaching, the deepest of them plumbing 2,300 feet below the summit of the main mine hill. The air down in that underworld must have been thin and cold and strange beyond imagining, and the reckoning of those two realms—cavern and tunnel and shaft below ground; redwood shack, live oak, clean sky, and chaparral above ground—was a difficult transition to tread day by day. The boundary was primarily crossed via the mine shaft. As Foote observed, "the bell strikes, the engineer moves a lever, the great wheels of the engine slowly swing round and the heads disappear down the black hole. I can see a hand waved and the glimmer of a candle for a little way. The spark grows fainter and a warm, damp wind blows up the shaft." Down below, the men worked ten- to twelve-hour shifts, six days a week, hacking cinnabar from the walls of the mountain-underground and hauling them up to the light to be heated to 1,200 degrees Fahrenheit in a giant furnace. There, cinnabar's ore emerged as a vapor that, when captured and cooled, became quicksilver—that substance of myth and legend, the original mercury, all gleaming and silver-dark—the only metal to remain liquid at room temperature. And these hills just south of the Santa Clara Valley were loaded with it, their bellies red with cinnabar and its secret quicksilver ore.

For millennia the cinnabar deposits had been known by local Ohlone people, who came to certain caves in the hills to gather the red dust for body paint. They traded it as far north as Washington. In the 1820s the rich red rock was discovered by local Mexicans working on José de los Reyes Berreyesa's Rancho San Vicente, but it wasn't until the 1840s that a full blown mining operation began. It was instigated by Andres Castillero, an officer of the Mexican Army, who knew that quicksilver was in high demand for the silver mines of Mexico, but was quickly taken over by the English industrial firm Barron, Forbes & Co. when Castillero was called away to service. When the gold rush enveloped California a few years later, New Almaden was an unexpected "bonzanza," as quicksilver was at that time essential for the refining of both gold and silver into their purest forms.

For its first fifteen years, virtually all labor at New Almaden was undertaken by Mexican hands, and the mining equipment, technology, and philosophy were

As part of their daily routine, miners descend one of New Almaden's shafts. Courtesy of the California Historical Society

Left: Firing up the smelting furnace for extracting quicksilver from cinnabar circa 1863.

Right: Weighing quicksilver at New Almaden.

Both photographs by Carleton E. Watkins and courtesy of the California Historical Society

all Spanish in origin—New (Nuevo) Almaden's name-sake, after all, was the famous Almadén quicksilver mine in Spain. Candles for the Virgin Mary burned in a rock hollow near one of the mine entrances, where men came to pray before going down, or after coming up, until Barron, Forbes & Co. sold the mine to an American firm in 1864.

The original Mexican settlement, which became known as Spanishtown, was a cluster of redwood houses across the low ridges, some on tall stilts with leaning balconies where bright potted plants grew in profusion, and morning glory vines twined up railings, where women sat in the late morning braiding their children's hair, and dust rose up in small clouds on the steep streets. At the height of its operation, Spanish-town housed as many as 1,500 miners and their fami-lies, mainly from Mexico and Chile.

In the early 1860s a new wave of labor arrived from Cornwall, where men had been mining tin as far back as the Bronze Age. The Cornish miners quickly established their own "Englishtown" on a separate set of ridges and hills, where, as Foote writes, "the camp

The Metal Pickers, from a Carleton E. Watkins stereograph circa 1867. Courtesy of the California Historical Society

Unidentified New Almaden miners. Courtesy of Santa Clara County Parks and Recreation Department

seem[ed] always to be washing or moving or both." The beginning of the settlement was marked by a wind-twisted coast live oak tree, remarkable for the many strange boxes affixed to its trunk, each inscribed with initials or other symbols to identify the owner; it was like a living post office, but instead of mail, the tree was the repository for various cuts of meat—soup bone, steak, leg of mutton—delivered regularly by the meat wagon.

The official post office was located in the central hacienda, the settlement that marked the entrance to the community of New Almaden, where neat cottages housed engineers and supervisors, and the palatial Casa Grande, residence of the mining company's owner and family, reigned over five acres of manicured grounds, lending an air of old European grandeur to the operation. From the mining camps up in the hills, the sight of the stagecoach full of letters laboring up the trail to the hacienda, "black leather curtains flapping in the wind, horses and driver covered in dust," must have been a welcome vision; those wheels and dusty horses bore

word from the outside world on their backs, precious as rain.

Water was always precious, and trains of mules led by aguadors in goatskin pants and broad hats hauled barrels of water up and down the trails daily between camps. By the 1870s, Chinese immigrants had set up tents and shacks in the brush and clearings between Spanishtown and Englishtown, finding work as both miners and laborers around the camps—doing laundry, chopping wood, cooking breakfast. Though miners met and mingled often in the evenings at the town's little cantinas, interracial tensions often simmered just below the surface, and the Chinese, as was the pattern throughout the Bay Area in the late nineteenth century, were often the scapegoats.

The mineworks in 1879. Courtesy of the California Historical Society

Opposite page, top: Miners' houses at New Almaden in 1917. Courtesy of the California Historical Society

Opposite page bottom: Miner's cabin near either New Almaden Mines or nearby Guadalupe Mines circa 1920s. Courtesy of Santa Clara County Parks and Recreation Department

Between 1846 and 1905, the peak years of New Almaden's operation, miners hauled up and processed millions of pounds of liquid mercury, making the mine the largest and richest in California's history. From 1850 to 1875 alone, 46 million pounds were carefully siphoned into 76-pound flasks for market. But such abundance, and such hubris—to play the divine alchemist, transmuting well-buried rock into a metal meant only for mountain veins and magma—were not without their cost. Mercury is incredibly toxic and doesn't break down once released into water and air; it simply cycles up and down through the food chain endlessly. Of the 84 million pounds of mercury produced by the mine during its 130 years of operation, it is thought that up to 17 million were left behind in the environment, either in the form of slag piles scattered around the camps, road bases built with some of the waste rock, dust dumped into the creeks, and vapors lost to the atmosphere during the heating process, which later worked their way into the soil. The New Almaden mine accounts for the vast majority of mercury in the San Francisco Bay today. It wasn't until the 1990s, decades after it closed, that the old mine was declared a Superfund site and open piles of waste and abandoned shafts were closed up, making it safe for the hikers, horseback riders, and bicyclists who now frequent its

trails and hills. During the intervening decades, poison had flowed freely from the hills south of San Jose down through the creeks and the Guadalupe River and into the bay: its algae, its zooplankton, its fish, its seals, its humans. By now, the mercury has flushed itself through the whole ecosystem and is slowly working its way out to sea.

Six miners pause their candlelit work at New Almaden circa 1865. Courtesy of Santa Clara County Parks and Recreation Department, Bulmore Family Collection

Six men and one large ore cart at the entrance to the main tunnel, hauling out a full load of cinnabar. At the far right is Sherman Day, who was mine superintendent during the 1860s. Photograph circa 1863 by Carleton E. Watkins. Courtesy of Santa Clara County Parks and Recreation Department

An illustration of Fort Ross in the 1840s by G. M. Waseurtz af Sandels. Courtesy of the California Historical Society

Fort Ross

Loshka, kushka, mishuk: these words are strange threads stitched through the quilt of the Kashaya Pomo language, left there by the Russians after they abandoned Fort Ross in 1841. Intimate, household words, variations of the Russian for spoon, cat, and dish, they hint at personal and linguistic entanglements, at simple mornings, lamp-lit evenings, and also the clash of two very different worlds. The Kashaya called the Russian settlers the Undersea People because they seemed to emerge one day right out of the ocean and up the shore, as if from beneath the waves themselves. When they left again, they vanished almost as suddenly as they'd appeared.

For twenty-nine years—from 1812 to 1841—a village of Russians, Alaska Natives, and California Indians thrived on the bluffs outside the redwood walls of Fort Ross, the Slavic-style fortress that housed the Russian-American Company on the Sonoma coast about seventy miles north of San Francisco. In the mornings the tide seethed high up the ragged cliffs beyond the fort, the air smelled of kelp and salt, and the black oystercatchers on the shore called out in high, clear voices. In the evenings the stars were a thick fur above the redwood

ridges, white and bristling, and all was quiet save the Kashaya campfires up in the hills, where laughter and the clatter of gambling bones rang out long into the night. Up in the hills to the east, an orchard of apples, pears, and peaches grew, and grapes flourished alongside them. Below the fort a lapis cove fed by a wide creek rocked and thrashed at high tide. There, a master Aleutian tanner turned the hides of cattle into boots, shoe soles, and other leather goods using a series of redwood vats and the bark of the tan oak, which was cut and crushed by two nearby windmills. The sound of clanging metal rang out from the blacksmith shops, flour mills processed wheat grown (rather poorly) in nearby fields, and the smell of fresh bread came hot on the air from the doors of the bakery. Inside the fort, Russian commanders, priests, and their families lived in neat redwood-walled houses built in the style of old Scandinavian stave churches: the aura of amber-dark wood, the elegantly peaked towers. Among the buildings within the fort walls were a chapel, a watch house, a blockhouse, and a warehouse, all of hand-hewn redwood and silvered with age.

Top: Inside the Russian church, with its low redwood ceiling and great round tower.

Bottom: The Russian church at Fort Ross in the late 1800s or early 1900s, after the Russians had left and the land was passed on to American settlers.

Left: A round house on the Fort Ross grounds.

All photographs courtesy of the California Historical Society

Half a dozen or more languages mingled in the long, sweet mesa grass, in the air between the Russian, Aleutian, Kodiak, Kamchatkan, and Siberian workers who lived outside the walls, many of whom had eagerly married local Kashaya Pomo women. It was likely these women who tucked the words for *sock* and *cat* and *dish* into the treasury of their language and taught them to their children. A French visitor in 1828 observed sixty Russians, eighty "Aleuts" (native Alaskans of various tribal affiliations), and eighty California Indians living peaceably together in the gentle meadowland beyond the walls of the fort. These men and women supplied most of the labor for the running of the place, and were paid reasonably in both money and company food and clothing. As one Fort Ross manager, Peter Kostromitinov, observed with some confusion in his 1839 report "Remarks on the Indians of Upper California," the Kashaya seemed to prize the clothing and other items their wages won them primarily as prizes to gamble away into the small hours of the morning with their friends. Games of chance and luck were highly valued in Kashaya culture, as across much of native California, where the circulation and fair distribution—rather than the accumulation—of material wealth was praised and celebrated.

Fur was the main business of Fort Ross. It was a long trail of fur that first brought Count Nikolai Rezanov to the San Francisco Bay and the hearth of its comandante Don José Argüello in 1806. Fur trapping and trading had extended the frontier of the Russian Empire deep into Siberia in the seventeenth and eighteenth centuries, to the very edge of the continent in Kamchatka, and across the Bering Strait to Alaska by the 1740s. Marten, ermine, red fox, blue fox, sable, wolverine, and finally, in the waters of the Pacific, sea otter—an endless appetite for their pelts paved the way. When a fur trading outpost in Sitka, Alaska, suffered a very hard winter in 1805, leaving its native Aleutian and Russian inhabitants starving and scurvy-ridden, Rezanov

An 1818 painting of Bodega Miwok Indians by Mikhail Tikhonovich Tikhanov during his stay at Bodega Bay and Fort Ross. The *Kamchatka* ship can be seen through the tule hut's door. From Scientific Research Museum, Russian Academy of Fine Arts. Courtesy of Fort Ross Conservancy

An "isba," a traditional Russian house, said to be like one seen in California by Eugène Duflot de Mofras during an 1841 visit. Courtesy of Fort Ross Conservancy

The Russian-American Company flag. From the Russian State Historical Archive. Courtesy of Fort Ross Conservancy

set out south for San Francisco immediately, desperate for a trade relationship with the Spanish Empire that would supply food to Russia's northern colonies. Rezanov found not only a gentle climate amenable to farming but also the coast and wild waters west of San Francisco teeming with harbor seals, fur seals, sea otters, sea lions, and elephant seals. A seasonal encampment was immediately erected on the Farallones to hunt them

Securing a trade agreement with Spain, the Russian-American Company built Fort Ross in 1812. Though outfitted with canons and an armed guard (there was some fear that the Spanish, not altogether pleased with the idea of Russian neighbors, might attack even though they had no claim to the land), the fort was at its core an agricultural endeavor. But as beautiful and

mild as Fort Ross's location was, neither the soil nor the commanders running the place, none of whom had any training or vocation as farmers, had much of a knack for growing wheat. Coastal fog, and an endless battle with gophers, blackbirds, and mice, didn't help matters. It was said that administrator Ivan Kuskov's garden yielded better than the neatly plowed fields of wheat; he tended it with a certain personal devotion, growing all sorts of vegetables, including beets and cabbages, which he liked to pickle. But despite dismal farming results, the Russians were resourceful and stubborn, and the gentle coastal air, sweet with wild grass and redwood and salt, quickly won hearts. One manager, Alexander Rotchev, later reflected that his years at Fort Ross, that "enchanting place," were the best of his life. And although agriculture was never the Russian-American Company's strong suit, the Russians stayed for three decades, turning instead to cattle-raising for tallow, skin, and meat, logging, tool-making, and lumbering. Before old-growth trees were logged at steam-powered mills in the Oakland hills, Fort Ross was also the primary supplier of redwood lumber for Mexican California. The Spanish in particular turned out to be eager trading partners, happy to travel up from the San Francisco Bay to get their hands on the Russian farming equipment, metalwork, barrels, and other tools produced at Fort Ross, which they weren't especially keen on having to make themselves.

Twenty miles off the coast of Fort Ross, Russians also hunted marine mammals from their base on Southeast Farallon Island. The Russian flag flew off the island's granite crags for almost half a century, but the community was never more than a huddled gathering of stone huts with roofs made of sea lion skin. Men cooked their meals over smoky, sputtering fires lit from sea lion bones soaked in their own oil, as the bare granite

View of Fort Ross in 1828 by A. B. Duhaut-Cilly. Courtesy of Fort Ross Conservancy

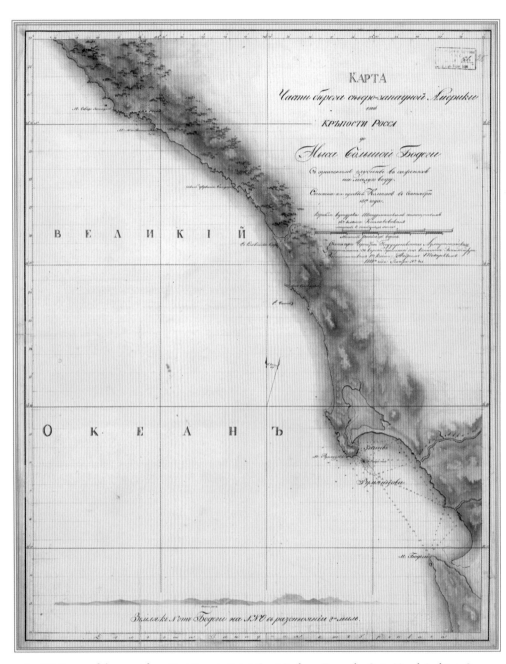

An 1817 map of the coast from Fort Ross to Point Great Bodega. From the State Naval Archive, St. Petersberg, Russia. Courtesy of Fort Ross Conservancy

peaks offered no wood for burning. Seal meat, seabird eggs, shellfish, and a few struggling turnips grown miraculously in a small garden plot, were the standard fare. Scurvy was common, and the weather so intense that the islands seemed to shake and moaned during storms.

Between seven and one hundred men lived on Southeast Farallon Island during the hunting season, trapping sea lions, fur seals, elephant seals, and otters in the wild and cold waters nearby. They used the sleek, fast Aleutian baidarkas to hunt in, harpooning so many sea mammals in a season that they left behind huge stinking carcass piles on the shore. A handful of Russian overseers lived on the island too, but mostly the community consisted of Kodiak, Prince William, Kamchatkan, Siberian, Aleutian, and California Indian men in the employ of the Russian-American Company, as well as their Kashaya wives. Often, men were sent to work on Southeast Farallon for some offense they'd committed against their Russian commanders at Fort Ross. The place was haunted with the ancient sorrows of slaughtered seals, and the sorrows of the men and women sent to work there. It was a soul-breaking job, to club to death a hundred sea lions and their pups. All in a day's work.

On the island, animals were processed into bundles of skin; cases of dried seabird, seal meat, and sea lion sinew; and kegs of blubber, all of which were shipped back to the mainland to be sent north to Sitka. Untold thousands of lustrous beings were killed and shipped to a distant coast in this way, their bones left behind in ghostly piles. The sea otters—with their astonishingly thick coats and their gentle, bobbing ways—once

Lukaria Yorgen Meyers, a Kashaya Pomo matriarch and oral historian who was a little girl at the time of the first arrival of the "Undersea People." Courtesy of Fort Ross Conservancy

The Russian stave church at Fort Ross in 1933, reconstructed after a fire to exactly resemble the original in materials and style. Courtesy of the California Historical Society

abundant in the kelp forests off the coast and in the San Francisco Bay, were virtually extinct by the 1830s, and with them went the giant kelp forests, which were rapidly consumed by the voracious purple-spined sea urchins that had once been the otters' main food.

By 1841, with all fur-bearing sea mammals in decline, and their agricultural efforts little improved, the Russians sold Fort Ross to the rancher John Sutter, on whose land gold would be discovered seven years later. When the Russians abandoned the coast of California and headed back to their various homes, from Sitka all the way to St. Petersburg, they left a grievous wound on the people left behind. Several Kashaya women and children were taken with their husbands, a source of great grief and heartache for the loved ones they left behind on the shore. What was worse (according to stories passed down from grandmother to granddaughter through the generations)—just before the Russians set sail, they raped two Kashaya girls, leaving behind a legacy of anger and violence. It took nearly two hundred years to gain some measure of reconciliation, when, in 2012, a delegation of Kashaya Pomo people traveled to Russia to see if they might trace the legacies of their female ancestors who journeyed there so many years before. They were met with respect and open arms. They were given private viewings of their baskets and other sacred artifacts that had been taken across the Pacific centuries before.

On the landscape, however, they left behind hardly a trace—an ancient apple orchard, some old redwood fortresses—and little more among the people: a few words, a lineage of light blue eyes, and the passed-down stories of the Undersea People, who came and went so quickly, taking with them a world and a time that would never quite return. To this day, Kashaya people and visiting Russians alike hold ceremonies in the reconstructed historic fort buildings. Whether they are Russian Orthodox Church services or traditional Kashaya dances, the land that briefly held the history of comingled cultures is still honored.

Settlement Ross in 1841, drawn by I. G. Voznesenskii. From Peter the Great Museum of Anthropology and Ethnography, Russian Academy of Science, Kunstkamera, St. Petersberg, Russia. Courtesy of Fort Ross Conservancy

Horses, cattle, and carts at the Mission Santa Clara de Asis, founded in 1777. Courtesy of the California Historical Society

Ranchos of the Santa Clara Valley

The approach to Rancho Posolmi from Mission Santa Clara in the year 1843 snakes along the Guadalupe River. It's a circuitous journey, bend after bend through wet meadows, past little ponds and bare-branched stands of willows that from a distance look like smoky flames. Geese are everywhere underfoot, great throngs of them that rise up, honking, when startled, in such vast groups their wingbeats create a wind that moves the manes of the horses. It's the rainy season and among the rushes the frogs are deafening. There is a sweet smell of mud, and the musk of alders and tules, and the drifting smoke of wood fires where women are cooking masa into thick corn tortillas. Where there are roads there are deep and muddy grooves from oxcarts, and the horses' hooves suck and slip. The fertile riparian valley of Santa Clara has to be taken at a walking gait, though the horses, raised by the Californios for skilled vaqueros, are jumpy and snorting with the itch for a good run.

To get to Lope Inigo's Rancho Posolmi—also called El Posada de las Ánimas (the Little Well of Souls)—a traveler must first pass the larger rancho of the imposing Don Ignacio Alviso and his fine adobe house. There, his wife and daughters

might be out on the porch if the day is fine, mantles over their dark and gleaming hair, red sashes around their waists and fine kidskin shoes flashing—despite the mud—under their heavy skirts. Hungry or weary or in need of a bed for the night, travelers are always treated with the utmost generosity, even given the hostess's bedroom to sleep in if there are no other free chambers. There, black-framed paintings of the saints preside over whitewashed walls, and fine Spanish trunks—raised off the ground to allow room for a broom beneath—loom in the corners, full of many folded linens. A fine, bright sombrero, newly woven, hangs from a peg on the wall. For supper, a steak, with ample tortillas and eggs and hot tea, are generously proffered.

According to a Californio custom of rather extreme machismo, men are always served the meat of bulls, not cows or calves. And there are certainly enough bulls ranging the hills to satisfy such hunger. The land is thick with cattle, and with an array of hardy, handsome horses. Don Ignacio, like other Californios, doesn't fence his horses but rather brands them and hitches a leather lasso around their necks that drags behind as they graze freely, until someone comes to their pasture to saddle them up for a ride. "The men usually catch one in the morning, throw a saddle and bridle upon him, and use him for the day, and let him go at night, catching another the next day," wrote Richard Henry Dana Jr. in his 1840 memoir *Two Years before the Mast*. "When they go on long journeys, they ride one horse down, and catch another, throw the saddle and bridle on him, and, after riding him down, take a third, and so on to the end of the journey. There are probably no better riders in the world."

The world of the vaquero in Mexican California, with his vast ranch holdings and his countless cattle, was a brief one—a quick flourishing of ranchos between the era of Spanish missionaries and the gold rush. The traces of it are few and far between. But in the 1830s and '40s, horses and cattle reigned supreme across California. Cowhides were traded at such a rate up and down the state (and overseas) that they were known as "California bank notes." Hides and tallow made up the economy of the ranchos. Vaqueros were celebrated in parades, fandangos, bullfights, and horse races, the horses just as excited as their masters by the low hum of the lasso as it whipped out to catch a bull. It was likely during these brief decades, with cows grazing up and down the state, that the composition of California's grasslands was transformed forever, perennial natives almost fully displaced by the aggressive European annual grasses that were brought over in the hooves and feed of Spanish cattle. During this era, almost all of the South Bay was parceled out in giant land tracts to a few prominent families, their long-horned cattle and horses turning marsh and tidal grassland into pasture. Before them, these ranchos belonged to the mission.

Mission Santa Clara was founded in 1777 and, like all missions in California, its pretext was to bring Christian civilization to what Spanish priests saw as a "childish" and "barbaric" native people. But this was always, at its heart, a colonial endeavor. Religion was just a way in. For the Spanish and then Mexican governments, teaching the native Ohlone people Spanish and converting them to Catholicism was as much about creating a stable workforce in Santa Clara and elsewhere as it was about salvation.

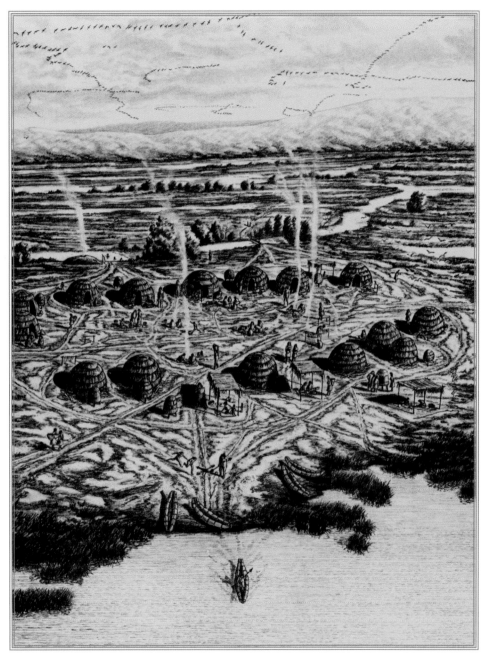

A traditional, precontact Ohlone village, as drawn by Michael Harney. From *The Ohlone Way*, by Malcolm Margolin, 1978. Courtesy of Heyday

Ohlone Indians at Mission San Jose preparing for a dance. Drawing by Georg von Landsdorff circa 1806. Courtesy of The Bancroft Library

Opposite page: California Indian hunting equipment and fine basketry circa early 1800s.

Both images courtesy of The Bancroft Library

To that end, mission neophytes were stripped of their traditional attire and given rough-spun wool shifts and habits. They were forbidden the foods they and their families had eaten for thousands of years. Women and men were sent to separate dormitories, and any expression of sexuality out of wedlock was severely punished, as were any attempts by women to abort their babies. Women were taught to spin wool and operate looms in order to weave fabrics needed for clothing, bedcovers, and other textiles. They were also set to work grinding grains—not the acorns or clarkia seeds they were used to, but new seeds: wheat and corn. Men were sent out into the fields to tend growing herds of cattle and sheep. The bells in the tower rang out on a strict schedule, and the days of Ohlone women, men, and children were molded by the dictates of the clock; it rang for sunrise prayers, for breakfast, for work, for noonday meal, for more work, for evening prayers and devotions, for supper, for bed. Anyone who did not adhere strictly to this schedule and to the rules of the mission was flogged; disobedience was met with shackles or the stocks.

Armes et ustensiles de Californie.

It was a horrendous arrangement for a people who had lived for thousands upon thousands of years within the gentle bounty of the Santa Clara Valley, wholly unfettered by clocks and crosses and totalitarian regimes. But for the Ohlone, their way of life began to change even before they were moved into the mission. When the first Spanish settlers arrived in the valley, these new settlers set their livestock free to roam at will; the herds of cows, horses, pigs, goats, and mules dramatically altered the ecosystem. Invasive annual grasses began to take over the wildflower-seed-rich meadows Ohlone people relied on for grain. By the 1790s, most Ohlone adults were flocking to the mission out of sheer hunger.

The missionaries' plan was to train native people to "usefully" cultivate their own land with corn, beans, and cows, and then return the land to them as legal, assimilated citizens of Mexico. But a few things got in the way, among them the greed of a rising class of Californio rancheros and the rampant spread of foreign diseases such as syphilis, smallpox, mumps, pneumonia, and measles to native people who had no natural immunity. By the time Mission Santa Clara was secularized in 1836 due to pressure from the restless Californios, who wanted the fertile tracts of mission land for themselves, Ohlone populations were much reduced, and severely discriminated against from all quarters. Only a few mission Indians were given any land at all.

Among them, eventually, was Lope Inigo, owner of Rancho Posolmi.

After being released from the mission in 1839 from what amounted to fifty years of glorified slavery, Inigo wasn't given any land. At age fifty-eight he simply

A portrait of Lope Inigo from 1860, with "Old Chief Ynigo of Mission Santa Clara, and later Ynigo's farm Mountain View" inscribed on the reverse. Courtesy of the Archives & Special Collections, Santa Clara University Library

left and began squatting on the swath of land with a creek and the hush of willows running through. There were two shellmounds—the remains of stable seasonal Ohlone villages that had been inhabited for millennia—on the site, one of them probably the village where Inigo was born. Not knowing what else to do, it seems that he went home.

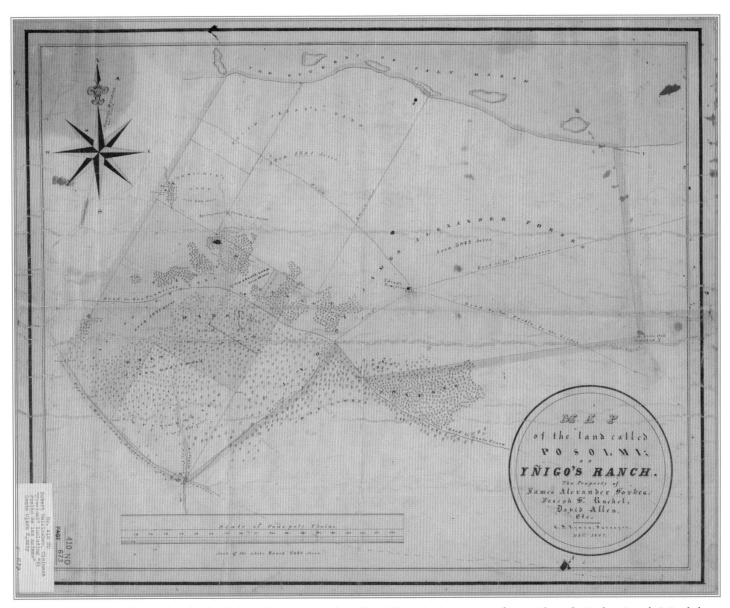

An 1847 hand-painted map of the land called Posolmi, or Inigo's (here "Yñigo's") ranch, the property of James Alexander Forbes, Joseph S. Ruckel, David Allen, etc., C.S. Lyman, Surveyor. Courtesy of The Bancroft Library

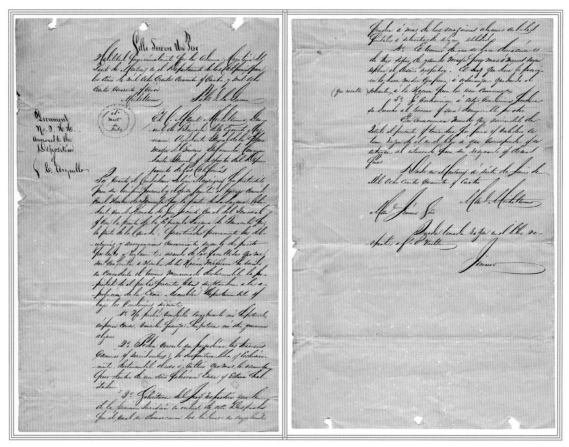

An example of a land grant issued by the governor of Mexican California in 1844 to one Julian Mauriquez in Riverside County for a property then known as Temecula. Courtesy of the California Historical Society

By that time, Inigo was a full Mexican citizen, fluent in Spanish and a devout Christian; he'd served as an alcalde (magistrate) in the mission for decades, commanding Indian neophytes on behalf of the priests. Immediately after building himself a small straw house and planting a few inaugural fruit trees, Inigo went through the traditional channels to secure his land grant. He first petitioned Prefect José Castro for official rights to the plot, appealing to Castro's humanity,

based on "all the services […] rendered" to the Crown during Inigo's long stay at the mission. Castro referred him directly to Governor Alvarado, whom Inigo visited in Monterey. Even so, it took five years for the government to officially grant Inigo his land. In the meantime, he turned the place into a thriving home economy, with a modest flock of sheep, herds of cattle, a loom for weaving wool, and several wooden and adobe houses, where both he, his second wife, and many of his adult

children lived. The lavish and sprawling world of the ranchos that he inhabited was itself a brief era, a quick flourishing of horse and cow before American gold rush settlers came flocking, and again changed the landscape of the Bay Area forever.

Inigo lived at Rancho Posolmi until his death in 1864, though by that time most of the land around him had been sold off to settlers from Europe and the United States. He had only a brief decade of freedom, but within it he could be his own person, as he had been as a little boy, unfettered by the everyday control of mission priests.

And so, as you continue the winding path to visit him in the year 1843, past Rancho Alviso, down through the fertile marshes of the Santa Clara Valley toward Rancho Posolmi, the mission comes into view. It is in disrepair, its whitewashed adobe walls are dull and peeling and the redwood posts going silver with age. The tall iron crosses and great bells in the belfry are deep orange with rust. Out front, the brush huts built by Ohlone residents are abandoned and caving in. Only a few caretakers are left, friars in threadbare gray habits and sandals that slap softly on the earthen floors, their heads shaved in the Franciscan manner.

When Rancho Posolmi at last comes into view from beyond a soft corridor of willows, it is dusk. The ranch is not as large as Alviso's; it's a humble three thousand acres (less than half the size of the lands of most non-Indian landowners), but the sheep grazing quietly on the new green are plump, woolly, and unconcerned, and the cows are lowing happily at the smells that evening brings up out of the earth. Smoke curls from the short chimney of a white adobe house. It is flanked by bare-branched apricot trees and a kitchen garden, now just beanpoles waiting for their summer vines. A man is on the porch, smoking a pipe. He's not big and imposing like Don Alviso, but there is a lean muscularity to him that bespeaks a life of hard labor. His eyes, though, tracing the fall of night from between the puffs of his pipe, are patient, and gentle, and bright with the many worlds they have seen come and pass away again.

A sketch of the Mission Santa Clara de Asis and surrounding lands by G. M. Waseurtz af Sandels. Courtesy of the California Historical Society

Acknowledgments

I'd like to thank Malcolm Margolin for dreaming up these many lost worlds and asking me to write a book comprised of them. Malcolm is a storehouse of stories and reflections, of histories and scraps of beauty unlike any you've ever encountered. He's more than a storehouse—he's a living vehicle of story, blooming wonderments, and memories that will make you weep and rejoice by turn.

I've heard Malcolm say many times how he is so often staggered by the beauty of the human spirit. That he chooses to let this give him hope, and pleasure, and joy. Thank you, Malcolm, for all the ways you have shared and imparted this philosophy to me and to so many others, and for the inspiration your friendship and mentorship have brought to my life.

For their generous help finding, acquiring, and scanning the images in this book, I'm grateful to the following individuals and institutions: Chris Adams and Bill Hoffland, The Bancroft Library, Berkeley Giclee (Tom Molatore), Bulmore Family Collection (Wes Lord), the family of John Caito Sr., California Historical Society (Debra Kaufman, Alison Moore, and Marie Silva), David Rumsey Map Collection, East Bay Regional Parks District (Kate Collins, Crystal Jimenez, and Brenda Montano), El Cerrito Historical Society (Tom Panas), Fort Ross Conservancy (Sarjan Holt), History San José, The Mark Twain Papers and Project (Melissa Martin), Mill Valley Public Library History Room (Cate Mayfield), Chuck Millar, Moraga Historical Society (Elsie M. Mastick), New Bedford Whaling Museum, Pat Hathaway Collection (Pat Hathaway), San Francisco History Center at San Francisco Public Library, San Francisco Maritime National Historical Park (Gina Bardi), Santa Clara County Parks and Recreation Department (Ann Laverty and Rhonda Southworth), Santa Clara University Archives (Sheila Conway), and Sausalito Historical Society (Jan Keizer, Roland Ojeda, and Sharon Seymour). Special thanks to David Deis for his beautiful map and to Igino Marini for the generous use of his font on the map.

I'd also like to thank Heyday's designer Ashley Ingram for her impeccable taste, immaculate vision, and joyous help on numerous archival fieldtrips to gather all of the images for this book. And of course to the whole brilliant Heyday team, whose vision and kindness are without peer; to David Plant, for his generous support of this project; and above all, to the landscapes, peoples, and histories of the beautiful, diverse, wildly storied Bay Area, land of my birth and my heart.

FURTHER RESOURCES OF NOTE

Point Molate Whaling Station

"America's Last Whalers," *Quest,* KQED Radio, March 2, 2007.

"Whaling from San Francisco Bay," *Bay Nature,* January–March 2003.

Marinship

Marinship Memories. Documentary film directed by Joan Lisetor.

"Marinship" exhibition. The Bay Model Visitor Center, Sausalito, CA.

Neptune Beach

"Neptune Beach" exhibition. The Alameda Museum, Alameda, CA.

Neptune Beach Revisited. Short film by the California of the Past digital storytelling project.

Fruit Orchards of the Santa Clara Valley

Chapman, Robin. *California Apricots: The Lost Orchards of Silicon Valley.*

Stanley, Tim. *The Last of the Prune Pickers: A Pre-Silicon Valley Story.*

Arequipa Pottery

Baizerman, Suzanne, Lynn Downey, and John Toki. *Fired by Ideals: Arequipa Pottery and the Arts & Crafts Movement.*

Belgum Sanitarium

Cole, Susan D. *Richmond—Windows to the Past.*

Bohemia at Monkey Block

Brook, James, Chris Carlsson, and Nancy J. Peters, eds. *Reclaiming San Francisco: History, Politics, Culture.*

The Emporium Department Store

Hendrickson, Robert. *The Grand Emporiums: The Illustrated History of America's Great Department Stores.*

Hitz, Anne Evers. *Emporium Department Store.*

The Mount Tamalpais and Muir Woods Railway

Graves, Al and Ted Wurm. *The Crookedest Railroad in the World: California's Mt. Tamalpais & Muir Woods Railroad.*

Steaming up Tamalpais. Short film directed by Cris Chater.

The Sand Dunes of Old San Francisco

Nolte, Carl. "Tombstones from long ago surfacing on SF Beach," SFGate, June 8, 2012.

Holloran, Pete. "The San Francisco Sand Dunes," FoundSF.

Mount Diablo Coal Mines

Parent, Traci and Karen Terhune. *Black Diamond Mines Regional Preserve.*

Black Diamond Mines Regional Preserve, Antioch, CA.

The Farallon Lighthouse

White, Peter. *The Farallon Islands: Sentinels of the Golden Gate.*

Paddlewheel Boats

Cunningham, Laura. *A State of Change: Forgotten Landscapes of California.*

MacMullen, Jerry. *Paddle-Wheel Days in California.*

Shrimp Fishing at China Camp

Ellinger, Mickey. "From the Bottom Up: The Tiny Bay Shrimp Makes History," *Bay Nature,* January–March 2002.

Museum at China Camp Village, China Camp State Park Museum, San Rafael, CA.

The Last Days of Oakland's Redwoods

Burgess, Sherwood D. "The Forgotten Redwoods of the East Bay," *California Historical Quarterly,* March 1951.

van der Zee, John. *Canyon: The Story of the Last Rustic Community in Metropolitan America.*

New Almaden Quicksilver Mine

Foote, Mary Hallock. "A California Mining Camp," *Scribner's Monthly,* February 1878.

Schneider, Jimmie. *Quicksilver: The Complete History of Santa Clara County's New Almaden Mine.*

Fort Ross

Bear, Lindsie. "To Russia With Love: A Kashaya Journey of Reconciliation," *News from Native California,* Fall 2013.

Farris, Glenn J. *So Far from Home: Russians in Early California.*

Fort Ross State Historic Park, Jenner, CA.

Ranchos of the Santa Clara Valley

Dana, Richard Henry, Jr. *A Yankee in Mexican California: 1834–1836.*

Milliken, Randall T. and Laurence H. Shoup. *Inigo of Rancho Posolmi: The Life and Times of a Mission Indian.*

About the Author

Sylvia Linsteadt was born and raised at the base of Mount Tamalpais in the San Francisco Bay Area. Her fiction and nonfiction is rooted in a deep sense of place, both human and ecological. Other works include *Wonderments of the East Bay,* coauthored with Malcolm Margolin, and the mythic novel *Tatterdemalion.* More about Sylvia and her work can be found on her website, www.sylvialinsteadt.com.

HEYDAY

About Heyday

Heyday is an independent, nonprofit publisher and unique cultural institution. We promote widespread awareness and celebration of California's many cultures, landscapes, and boundary-breaking ideas. Through our well-crafted books, public events, and innovative outreach programs we are building a vibrant community of readers, writers, and thinkers.

Thank You

It takes the collective effort of many to create a thriving literary culture. We are thankful to all the thoughtful people we have the privilege to engage with. Cheers to our writers, artists, editors, storytellers, designers, printers, bookstores, critics, cultural organizations, readers, and book lovers everywhere!

We are especially grateful for the generous funding we've received for our publications and programs during the past year from foundations and hundreds of individual donors. Major supporters include:

Advocates for Indigenous California Language Survival; Anonymous (3); Judith and Phillip Auth; Carrie Avery and Jon Tigar; Judy Avery; Dr. Carol Baird and Alan Harper; Paul Bancroft III; Richard and Rickie Ann Baum; BayTree Fund; S. D. Bechtel, Jr. Foundation; Jean and Fred Berensmeier; Joan Berman and Philip Gerstner; Nancy Bertelsen; Barbara Boucke; Beatrice Bowles; Jamie and Philip Bowles; John Briscoe; David Brower Center; Lewis and Sheana Butler; Helen Cagampang; California Historical Society; California Rice Commission; California State Parks Foundation; California Wildlife Foundation/California Oaks; The Campbell Foundation; Joanne Campbell; Candelaria Fund; John and Nancy Cassidy Family Foundation; James and Margaret Chapin; Graham Chisholm; The Christensen Fund; Jon Christensen; Cynthia Clarke; Lawrence Crooks; Community Futures Collective; Lauren and Alan Dachs; Nik Dehejia; Topher Delaney; Chris Desser and Kirk Marckwald; Lokelani Devone and Annette Brand; J.K. Dineen; Frances Dinkelspiel and Gary Wayne; The Roy & Patricia Disney Family Foundation; Tim Disney; Doune Trust; The Durfee Foundation; Michael Eaton and Charity Kenyon; Endangered Habitats League; Marilee Enge and George Frost; Richard and Gretchen Evans; Megan Fletcher; Friends of the Roseville Public Library; Furthur Foundation; John Gage and Linda Schacht; Wallace Alexander